Private Collection: Amore Normale

Private Collection:
Amore Normale

SILVIA OLLA

Cover designed by Valeria Pola

2017

First Printing: 2017
ISBN 978-1-387-05903-4
Silvia Olla
Singapore

This book is available in Ebook format.

To Giorgio, Luciana and Marcella.

CONTENTS

Preface ix

ALIVE 1
18 SQUARE METERS 6
BITTERSWEET 12
CHAMPAGNE CONNECTION 21
CLOUDS 26
CONVERSATION 34
DIRTY LITTLE SECRET 44
DREAM 50
FLIGHT OR FRIGHT 53
FREEDOM FROM ME 57
FULL MOON 61
ITALIAN 69
KARMA 75
MEANT TO BE 79
NO PLANS 91
OBSESSION 95
THIS COULD BE FOREVER 102
PINOT NOIR 105
REAL VALUE 114
RULES 118
SELF LOVE 125
SHE'S THE ONE 129
TO BE CONTINUED 136
TOO EARLY 149
WAR AND PEACE 155
Acknowledgments 161

Preface

I had been living in Singapore for just over two years when I started collecting these stories.

It was during a time when my perspective was shifting, and I wanted to concentrate on the things and people who really mattered, the ones worth keeping, the ones who brought depth and meaning to my life.

Eventually, this led to a passionate search for authenticity in everything I had accumulated over the years: relationships, passions, memories, the worries that kept me up at night and the thoughts that drove me during the day.

Going through every object, card, gift and photo, I felt the increasing need to pause and savour one of the simplest yet most beautiful feelings within the human experience: romantic love. As part of my quest, I approached people and asked them to share the life experiences that have shaped their unique perspectives of this timeless and undefinable emotion.

Private Collection: Amore Normale, or normal love in Italian, is a special anthology of life stories and love stories, compiled as my personal tribute to love. Featuring people from different ages, backgrounds and places around the world.

A special thanks to all the contributors who gave of their time and stories so generously. Names and locations have been changed to protect the individual identities.

Let, *Love rule without rules & Love! Love until the night collapses!* - Thomas More & Pablo Neruda

Enjoy.
With Love,

Silvia

ALIVE

I am in pain today.

Last night, a very good friend of mine shared something with me that broke my heart. I didn't want her or anyone else to know how much I was hurting, so I pretended that I was totally cool with what I heard. I kept drinking. I kept laughing and asking people about their weekend plans. While my mouth kept smiling, my mind was flooded by thoughts of the betrayal.

When I got home afterwards, I switched on some music, changed and fell asleep, hoping that I would forget everything that happened by the time I woke up.

I didn't.

But despite how love could cut into me like it did, again and again, I found myself wanting to hold on to and keep alive the beautiful memories and feelings that it brought into my life. Despite how others could hurt me with

1

their actions, I would never change or give up on love and how much it meant to me. I wanted my heart to be strong but not hard or hopeless.

So I got dressed, left the house and cycled to a bar to meet a friend.

@anatomy of love

Love makes you feel alive. It is a feeling that could last forever or only as long as a single breath.

You could fall in love at first sight or first scent, when you smell someone. You can fall in love without even realising it. It is a chemical reaction, unstoppable, leaving the mind behind. Neither you nor your body can do anything about it.

It starts in my stomach like a slow burn and it does not matter how long the sensation lasts. What matters more is the intensity of the feeling. It is not how long but not how much it makes you feel alive.

Love exists in many different forms, unbound by time or place. One of my best friends, she fell in love with her husband the minute she saw him. Then there is the beautiful story of my grandparents, who have been in love with each other for 50 years and counting. The grandmother of my best friend fell in love with a lovely gentleman who lived in the same retirement facility. She is 85 years old.

It comes and goes. It lives and dies. It evolves with life. After a long time spent being with someone, the feelings change and love becomes something different from what you started with. The thought that an intense love could fade and be replaced by something more like friendship – that scares me.

Perhaps that is why people nowadays are drawn to the quick, intense satisfaction of temporary gratification. Pleasure now and not later. No one has the patience to wait. Better to experience momentary passion than eternal love because who knows what that will become?

From what I see, real love is something organic. It grows and regenerates, becoming something much bigger than a sentiment, a whole that is bigger than the sum of two individuals. This happens when, for example, families are formed and when children are born. But it takes time to build and effort to maintain. After all, instant gratification will only give you so much.

Many people entertain the idea of The One, that there is a perfect partner out there waiting to be found, who is exactly right for you in all the ways you expect, right from the start. Many of my friends abandoned their relationships because their partner did not turn out to be the person whom they, their families or their friends had expected.

That is just plain silly.

The hardest question is not about finding love but about keeping it. Specifically, how do you keep it alive? There is no universal answer. The women in my family are very independent and, unlike before, they work hard at their own jobs and they do not stick to their husbands. Still, they have found a way to keep love alive and keep their relationships.

It is more and more a struggle for people to combine the lives that they desire as individuals with the life they desire *together*. When love brings together two people of dramatically different backgrounds, there will be sacrifice. But how much of myself and my desires can I sacrifice for someone? Should I?

If I give up my dreams, I am no longer me.

Who will you love then?

18 SQUARE METERS

When I was living in Paris, I attended a party organized by a guy from school. The wine was cheap, the crowd was noisy and the place was a mess. I managed to find a quiet corner to sit and drink. He joined me and it might have been the free flow of drinks but we ended up talking and flirting all night. When I got up to leave, my friend Anna gave me a little nudge to get his number. "Why not? He's a nice guy."

So I decided to take a leap of faith. In Paris, that means something.

We started dating.

Life was good. I was living in a student apartment and I still remember the coziness of the place, all 18 square meters of it. It was a small space but I had everything I needed. I was in a university I had always dreamt of attending in a beautiful city I loved, surrounded by interesting people from around the world. My family would come visit and we would walk around town or lie down on the grass by the Eiffel Tower on a clear, sunny day. I felt like the luckiest girl.

After three weeks, he moved in with me and for three amazing years, those 18 square meters became our world and it never felt bigger.

At that time, my cousin was living on the same floor but in a bigger apartment and when they left, we happily moved in. For the first time, we had a proper bedroom that was separate from the living room. We did not have any money to buy furniture or even a fridge. In the winter, we would keep cheese outside the window to chill so we could eat it later!

One of my best girlfriends took over our cozy apartment and we could chat whenever we wanted, even from the window which connected both our bathrooms.

Although we barely owned anything and the apartment was practically empty, those were some of the happiest days of my life. I felt as if nothing could go wrong or even if it did, there was nothing I could not do or handle. I desired nothing more than what I already had and it was a great feeling.

Even now, ten years later, I still remember that feeling and the memory of that sensation is sharply imprinted on my mind and heart. I close my eyes and immediately I return to my apartment where we were 10 years ago, every detail intact.

He was tall, mysterious, very fit and very handsome. Wherever we went, girls would eye him with desire and guys would eye him with envy. While we were having dinner one night, he received a message from someone. She was an incredibly beautiful South American singer with whom he was collaborating on a new project.

I was jealous.

I became dramatically emotional and told him how affected I was by her presence, how insecure I felt. If the person I am with made me feel safe and comfortable, I would not feel this way. He understood.

Some people I know get hung up on details and they end up lost in the sea of things that frustrate them. I decided I wanted to focus on the bigger picture, on the things that told how lucky I was and how loved.

Between the both of us, I was always the more passionate and impulsive one. He was always more of a thinker. We had our ups and downs of course but I knew that we would always be there for each other. No matter what.

I remember one particular disagreement we had. I woke up the next morning and found him gone. All of a sudden, I thought of a world without him and my heart stopped. I never felt so terrible as I did then.

Later, I found out that he had walked for hours and eventually slept on the streets. He needed to think, he said.

When he finally returned, we spent the whole next day making up. We could not bear to keep our eyes and hands off each other, and spent our passion in the bedroom, the bathtub, on the sofa, in the kitchen. Without using words, we expressed the intensity of how we felt for each other. I could see the truth in his eyes and all the things he could not or would not say. My grandmother was right. She told me that the truth can always be found when you look right at someone in the eye.

Ironically, this was also how I later found out something was wrong. He did not mention anything but I knew that something had changed. Something had happened to his family. I did not know the details but I knew there was money involved and it was serious.

For the first time, I was left on the outside. He had drawn a tight circle around himself and I could not enter without getting hurt. For us, this was the beginning of the end. We tried to work around it at first. We took a trip to the Maldives and while it was amazing, I knew it was too late.

Years have passed since then and I dated many other guys after him but I could not find the same kind of relationship that we had together during those Parisian days. It was once and no more.

Even knowing that I would suffer for my decision, even if I could go back in time, I would not do things differently. What I fear more than getting hurt is the complete absence of love, leaving me nothing than an empty shell.

So I choose love – along with the possibility of pain, fear and loss. I choose love, over and over, always.

BITTERSWEET

When I am in love, it consumes me. I find myself wanting to spend all my time only with that person. I believed that love is about putting someone else before yourself and taking care of his interests before your own. He became the filter for all my decisions and everything I experienced, good or bad.

It has been 10 years since I felt that way. And it terrifies me to admit the absence in my life of someone to love because I know how beautiful an experience it is.

Perhaps I have become too good at protecting myself and in doing so, I've learned to be alone, to like myself and to be enough for myself without needing another person. I discovered that you can train your mind and your body to be independent, to live without love, and the heart to not feel it.

I am not sure if this means I am happy or simply used to it. If this is ever something you could get used to.

@laws of attraction @not everything that shines is gold

When I was much younger, I fell in love with an extremely gorgeous guy. He was so handsome that wherever we went – restaurants, cinemas, on the street, girls would turn their heads to look. They just couldn't help it. Neither could I.

We both had very strong personalities. I was stubborn and opinionated, and so was he. We would spend hours fighting and arguing but we also had a lot of passion between us. It was the passion and tension that made us feel alive.

Although we were dealing with a long distance relationship across two different cities – I was in Paris while he was in Morocco, distance was never an issue. We would talk every day, sharing our respective experiences, feelings and thoughts. We were physically apart but emotionally and mentally close, and we were happy. We even had a long-term plan, I was supposed to return as soon as I finished my internship and this plan kept us happy, passionate and full of hope.

But no one is perfect, neither he nor I. One of the biggest complaints people had about him was that he was a heavy smoker. He loved marijuana. I didn't mind much because whenever he was high, he would be more loving and tenderer with me. He would call with sweet nothings. He would be calm and patient. He would be more perfect that he already was.

My family and friends kept telling me that he was not the right person for me but we did not care. He did not give a shit what others thought and simply did what he thought was the right thing. He lived by his own rules. And I was just completely in love. I just attributed their warnings to a form of possessiveness and overprotectiveness that is typical of most families. In reality, they probably saw the truth more clearly than I did.

One February, I decided to surprise him for his upcoming birthday by making a trip to see him in Morocco. I knew he didn't like celebrating birthdays but I was so sure that seeing me would make him so happy, he would change his mind about how he felt.

I was broke and it took me a while to save enough but I bought my flight tickets without thinking twice.

At Charles De Gaulle, I bought him a birthday present – a beautiful leather belt from a well-known French brand. At my instructions, the salesgirl wrapped it up with the most gorgeous wrapping paper and it looked amazing. I could not wait to give it to him. More than that, I could not wait to see him and hug him tight.

As it turned out, I was the one surprised instead. I arrived to find him having sex with another girl.

Some people say that if you can forgive things like that, it makes a relationship stronger. I was not one of those people. I could not stand it and I could not forgive him. So I did the only thing I could do – I moved on.

@reset

A few months later, my internship in Paris ended and I decided, with bittersweet feelings, to move back to Morocco. I ended up sharing an apartment with one of my best friends to save money. He was nice, interesting and intelligent but we never got together.

We came home drunk one night after intense partying and I was so wasted, I had no idea what was going on. When he started having sex with me, it felt like I was in a dream and my real self was somewhere far way. Moments later, I sobered up and with a sudden clarity, realised that he was really in love with me and that I did not feel the same. I tried to push him away but he gently persuaded me to just enjoy the moment and let him express his love. I was touched by his warmth and his tenderness, and I stopped resisting.

From that night onwards, we developed a sex-love relationship. For him it was love but for me, it was just sex. He was loving, caring and sweet but I felt nothing. For the first time, I felt like the bad one in the relationship. I often hear people say that this is fun because you hold the power and are less likely to get hurt. If this was supposed to be fun, why did I feel like shit? Still, I was not brave enough to break up, so I looked for an excuse to leave by applying for a summer job overseas.

Eventually, he came to visit me in Italy and one night, over a takeout dinner of caprese salad, I broke up with him.

I kept looking and while it seemed like I was getting closer to finding the love I was looking for, it also felt like things kept getting in the way. It was either that the guys I liked were not in love with me or the other way round. I could not figure out what was wrong but nothing worked out.

Perhaps it was fate or karma but I ended up in yet another complicated relationship. We were together for four years and during that time, he asked me to marry him. I was surprised but instead of feeling happy, I felt insecure, unsafe and disoriented as if I got thrust into the spotlight without warning.

In short, I said no.
I just could not picture being with him or having a life with him. All I could think of were all the reasons why I could NOT marry this man. For him, work always came first and before I did. He had no regard for safety – his or mine, and would drive recklessly all the time. He never agreed to take a HIV test

although I had asked him to because I knew he was a heroin user before we met. It never seemed like my feelings or wellbeing was ever important to him.

Many women believe that they can change their partners for the better, bringing them closer to our idea of perfection. I did too. Because he did not want to have kids, I tried to convince myself that I was fine with it. Later, I realised that I could not live with this compromise at all. I wanted so, so much to have children and I had hoped that he would change for the better for my sake, for the sake of our children. Four years of hoping changed nothing.

@deep breath

The phone rang.
"Miss De Rossi?"

"Yes?"

"Your contact was given to us by a man who claims he is your partner. He is in jail and would like to know if you can come and pick him up."

That was pretty much the end of it.

At that point, it seemed as if life could not get any messier with an ex-boyfriend in jail and my self-confidence in pieces. I decided to leave my hometown for somewhere I could start over.

One evening, I stopped at a bar after work for a beer before heading home. While I sat there, a guy approached me and said, "I don't know you but I kinda like you."

At first, I just laughed it off. But a part of me felt a vague feeling I could not describe and that evening, I went home thinking about him.

There are some people we meet in our lives who will leave a deeper impression than others. There is an almost electrical tension, an unspoken connection that, once formed, is impossible to break. They hold our attention and stay in our thoughts.

That was what happened and it was obvious, inevitable, to both of us that we would start dating. He was charming and gentle, and he came into my life at the perfect moment with the love I needed to rebuild my confidence and emerge from my most fragile state.

By this time, I was also wiser and more mature. The strong connection we had made it communication easier and expectations clearer. Our time together was passionate, intense and loving. Everything was perfect except for a couple of things.

He was married. And also, our skin colour was different.

So we hid love from everyone we knew and we could not tell anyone. No one would ever approve of us – not my dad, my family, my friends or society and I did not have the strength to fight for us. So I ended it.
It took me more than four years to get over it and till today, I have not found anything that has even come close to what we had.

CHAMPAGNE CONNECTION

@unspoken words @connection @XY

X

Love is Passion. Reliability. Trust. Knowing that the other person will be there for you.

It is the absence of judgment, a complete acceptance, an unwavering trust. With her, I feel safe and comfortable with who I am.

Love is built upon appreciation and support; it grows with mutual admiration and shared passions.

It is a connection between one soul and another. Without uttering a single word, each person understands what the other is thinking.

But connecting with someone is only the beginning. What you do next is often more important than the discovery itself, whether you invest in it or let it fade.
As a young person years ago, I did not realize how valuable love was, taking advantage of it

and hardly caring. But that has changed over time.

As I grew older and the years passed, I discovered how incredibly difficult it was to find real love. And when you find it, it makes you want to do everything in your power to hold on to it and not let go.

Starting all over again each time also requires so much effort. I have so many friends who are still looking for love, desperate for that connection with someone yet sadly unable to find it.

When I think about love now, there is only one person – her face, her features, her voice - who comes to mind. I found my connection with her.

She has become such a constant presence in my life that I feel as if something is missing whenever she's not around. When she's not by my side, I find myself constantly looking for her with my eyes, my mind, my body.

Y

Love is when two people come together to grow a dream. Despite differences in age or any obstacles, the connection comes naturally. The more mature both are, the more connected, stronger the bond.

It is a trust that evolves and grows along with the goals that are shared. This becomes the unspoken bond that forms the context of a life together.

A relationship like that takes time, across a process of balancing, adjusting and learning from mistakes followed by unconditional acceptance.

I don't believe in love at first sight. That is only passion and physical attraction, not love. Love comes afterward and only if you are willing to let it in.

**@croissants @conversation
@a champagne connection**

X: We met via one of those social networking apps. Nowadays, that seems to be the only way to meet new people.

We were messaging each other often but only arranged to meet up after a couple of weeks. I decided to fly to the other side of the world to see her.

Y: I invited her to a champagne and cheese place. That night, we were so excited to see each other that we ended finishing three bottles of champagne. We brought the last bottle, half full, to the place of one of my friends.

Later that night, we headed to Jamie Oliver's restaurant for dinner. It was summer and the weather outside was perfect. When we were done, she called for a tuk-tuks to head back to her hotel and although what I really wanted was to take her back to my place, I knew she wanted me to go with her and I could not say no.

On the way there, my passion overcame me and I could not keep my hands off her, kissing her and reaching for her dress.

X: I was trying hard to be conservative and hold back but in the end, we did spend the night together. :)

The next morning, I woke up to the sounds of her moving around and when I asked her,

"What's going on?", she said, "Oh I'm going to buy a croissant."

Y: I was actually trying to escape. The fact is, I knew that the neighborhood bakeries were closed in the morning!

X: She has a lot of pride and does not like sleeping at another person's place. I can understand that.

That was the beginning of a two-year long-distance relationship. Living in two different time zones, we would each sleep with Skype on just so that we could stay connected throughout our days and nights.

Each morning, if she was still sleeping when I woke up, I would say to her across our screens, "Have a good day my love." before heading out to start the day. Every three weeks, we would meet face to face and I looked forward to it all the time.

Eventually, we decided to move to the same city and live together, so that was what we did, along with getting married and celebrating the moment with 50 of our dearest friends, family and 50 bottles of champagne no less!

CLOUDS

Love – for me – has evolved over time. When I was younger, it was all about passion, passion and more passion. All the memories I have of those years are of wild, uncontrollable emotions. I feel no shame in admitting that it was my emotions which were controlling me and my relationships, and not the other way around. That's just who I am.

I believe in immersing myself in all my relationships, even with friends. No grey areas and nothing vanilla in life for me. There is no soup without salt is what I think. Do it with passion or don't do it at all – that is who I am and how I live.

I love being in love – immersing myself in a sense of companionship and pure joy.

In my life, I have been lucky enough to experience love twice. Although they were both different kinds of relationships, both times it felt like I was walking on clouds. Lifted up and free.

@unexpected

I was in the US, attending an MBA programme which, unsurprisingly, drew a very international crowd. I had classmates from Europe, Asia, America, Africa.

I remember that day clearly, even though it has been ten years since. He walked into the classroom and I immediately did a double take, along with all the girls in class. He was clearly the most attractive guy in class.

When the course ended, we gather in Singapore to celebrate our graduation. It was an elaborate affair, held at a rooftop bar with live music, cocktails and a fancy dress code. There were hundreds of guests and plenty of alcohol.

It might have been the free flow of drinks but everyone was mingling, flirting and increasingly letting go of their inhibitions. I am not sure what happened but in a split second, I was thrown into the pool, fully dressed.

There was silence all round and it felt like the longest few seconds in my life.

All of a sudden, he leaps into the pool with his clothes on and swam towards me, holding my gaze with an intensity that made me feel as if we were the only two people left on the planet.

That night, I felt fantastic.

He was unlike the kind of guys I typically dated. I liked guys who were confident, arrogant even. The ones who like to run the show and be in the limelight. The ones who know their appeal and play with your feelings.

He was anything but. And I guess life is sometimes unexpected that way.

@declaration @expectations

A few months after we started dating, we decided to take a trip to Sri Lanka with the rest of our MBA classmates.

One drunk evening while we were there, I turned to him and said, "I love you."
He remained silent.

I felt a stab of disappointment. I was expecting him to reply without hesitation those same three words.

Expectations, the worst affliction on society if there ever was one. They ruin everything.

Eventually, he explained that it meant a lot to him to say those words to someone and to him, it was a real milestone that had as much significance as getting married. He said that it will happen but he just needed more time. There was nothing I could do then but to accept it.

Meanwhile, I was posted to Spain for work. I said yes because I liked the idea and the challenge of relocating to a new city. He came to visit me several times and one day – a day that was no different from any other, he said to me, "I love you."

The next few months flew by and they were amazing. I would spend a weekend in Barcelona, another in London and another in France. His family was incredible and he was a true gentleman. No matter where we went or who we met, he only had eyes for me.

A while later, my parents came to visit and it was the perfect opportunity to introduce him to them but I wanted to do that only if I knew he was The One. I told him what I felt and again, I sensed the same hesitation from him when I first told him I loved him. I could not go through the pain of uncertainty again, so I told him if he could not decide then, it meant that he did not want to spend the rest of his life with me.

I walked away then. And I will regret it to the day I die.

@weight

I started over in London. New city, new life, new firm, new love.

There was a guy in my team who had a level of energy that was hard to ignore. Each time he stepped into the room, he brought a distinct energy with him and everyone felt it. He was confident and incredibly attractive.

But I ignored any connection I thought existed between us, thinking it was nothing more than a casual attraction. Months pass and one day, something changed. Someone asked a question and we both answered at the same time, in the exact same way without thinking. When we looked at each other and laughed, something fell into place.

We had dinner together some time after that and we ended up talking for hours about everything from silly, inconsequential things to those that went deeper like the stuff we feared in life. We talked about business, family, life, dreams, religion, politics, nature and all the things we believed in.

WhatsApp was the magic that kept us going. Like two kids exploring the world for the first time, we spent countless hours chatting on WhatsApp and the more we talked, the stronger and deeper our connection grew.

That year, I decided to spend New Year's Eve in Brazil, where we were both separately sent to for work. That night, we spent two hours in my hotel room – talking. Being with him was one of the best times of my life and I felt emotions I never did before, a connection so strong that everyone around us could sense it as well. He would finish my sentences and he could read me like no one else could.

It was felt almost too good to be true. And it was.

He told me he was married.

He had married his wife many years ago, when he was 25, when he did not know any better. Meeting me changed his life and opened his eyes to the realisation that there was no longer any love left in his marriage and it has been that way for years now. I did not know what to think but I know I did not want to be this person for him.

He decided to tell his family, who reacted as you would expect anyone in this situation would. People thought he was having a mid-life crisis and no one took his feelings seriously. Even his wife. She thought our relationship was a passing phase, one that would eventually end with nothing more than a bitter memory weighing on the mind.

And so it did.

His company sent him to India and right in the middle of this emotional hurricane, he left.

In the end, we were left with only a bittersweet memory, one that lay heavy at the back of my mind.

CONVERSATION

Love is an innate physical connection. When I feel like my heart clenching and my head spinning. I don't know how it starts, only that I cannot control it as it grows and changes with time, people and situations.

Love is also an active choice, like happiness. It is a decision between two people, requiring trust and effort to make happen. Sometimes, it is also a kind of egotistical indulgence, when one forgets the consideration of the other, desperately and greedily taking without giving.

♠: Love is much more about joy. Being in love is to laugh! But when I was young it was exactly the opposite – everything was a drama!

♦: You learn through experience. You have to fall and get hurt in order to realise that pain is something you don't want to ever experience again, so you do everything in your control to avoid it.

Psychologically, many people are driven by the need to achieve certain things. When I was a teen, my life was a continuous series of milestones. First I had to find a boyfriend, go on dates, then holidays together.

But then, real life happened. And strangely enough, it sets you free not to be governed by these predefined milestones and life becomes so much more enjoyable. I can't even believe that I'm past 30 now. When I was 20, I thought that by 30, I would own a car, a house and have a family.

Society influences a lot of the choices we make, like a river current that pushes you along a certain path. Biology, too, limits us in our choices on when to have children for example. But there are no deadlines when it comes to love. It happens when it happens, filling up the holes in your life when you are ready and that was it for us.

@braccetto

♠: It all started when I invited my friend Olivia out for a drink to celebrate my promotion.

♦: My friend Olivia and I had planned a night out at Circolo Arci in Milan and I was supposed to stay at her place after that as I lived far from the city centre. That night, I was late in meeting her and so decided to call but when I did, I heard a guy's voice on the other end and he shot out, "Where the hell are you?"

"You're not Olivia."

He said, "No I'm Cesare. Nice to meet you over the phone. Anyway, we don't believe that you are simply taking a new route to get here. You are way too late!

♠: She was going to meet us at Colonne, San Lorenzo. When she arrived, I introduced myself without hesitation. "Hello I am Cesare! By the way, what do you think of my leather jacket? My dad didn't want to buy it for me, so I got it for myself at Forte Dei Marmi in Italy. Now, I would like to buy you girls a Sbagliato drink!"

♦: We then went to a place called CUORE and he did in fact buy us a drink called "Sbagliato", which was basically a very strong cocktail that gave you a huge kick in the stomach.

When I first met him, I thought he was gay, which is why I thought nothing of putting my arm under his as we made our way out later. In Italian, this is termed "braccetto" and it's common for best friends to walk affectionately in this manner.

At the end of the evening, ended up exchanging business cards in typical Milanese fashion and parted ways. I was a little disappointed he said nothing more.

The next morning, as I was making pancakes at Olivia's place, the doorbell rings and there was Cesare standing in the doorway. He invited himself in, called his mum and started telling her that I was making the best pancakes he'd ever seen. Olivia woke up then and we all sat and had breakfast together almost like we were a family.

Life went on after that and a few months later, we were all invited to a friend Beatrice's birthday party at Bobino. Everyone is in a party mood and energy levels were high. But

Cesare was late. And he was the only person I really wanted to see and talk to. He finally arrived and we all moved to another club. The second we got in, before I knew what I was doing, I made a move towards him.

What happened next was completely unexpected. He abruptly told me, "I have to go." and left me standing there while he escaped as fast as he could into the night.

At that time, I had no idea what I did wrong, at least to provoke such an extreme reaction. After 72 hours of silence, he finally texted me to invite me for a drink.

♠: To be very honest, I made my way from Brescia all the way to Milan in order to tell her that I did not want to meet with her anymore. I had intended to tell her that I was not looking for anything serious.

@openness

Sforzesco Castle, Milan. Lights all around, casting a spotlight on the fountain.

♠: "Do you usually dress like that to the gym?" I asked her.

♦: In reality, I did go to the gym. But after that I spent 30 minutes on showering and makeup, getting ready to completely mesmerise him. I didn't tell him that of course and just said "Yes, of course I did!", sounding miffed that he didn't believe me.

♠: We went to a nice wine shop close to Farini Street and made ourselves comfortable or as much as we could with the tension that we both felt. "So what happened on Friday? I'm not sure I understand what happened…"

♦: I could see the terror in his eyes as if he got bitten by something poisonous. He was afraid. I felt I had to do something.
"I really like you and I don't want to walk away from this. I believe that there is something real between us and I want to discover what it is."

I don't know exactly what happened after that but the night ended with a kiss in his Fiat 500 as the music played and the night wind stayed warm. I let him kiss me without doing anything dramatic and we agreed to see each other again.

Our next date was at Cesare's favourite seafood restaurant in town where he had booked a table. I was sick but I went anyway because I wanted to see him. On the way out at the end of the evening, we bumped into two of Cesare's closest friends at the entrance. On hindsight, it was suspiciously coincidental but I was too sick to notice anything that night.

Months later, Cesare would confess that he had called his friends there so that they could see the girl he was spending time with. I suppose you could say that this was the start of our love story.

@couple @Einaudi

Were we in a relationship or were we just dating casually? A serendipitous development forced us to confront the decision. Cesare was leaving Milan for another city to work and we had to decide what we meant to each other.

That weekend, we went to IKEA and ended up buying a queen-sized mattress of all things.

To me, that was clear sign that marked the start of something serious.

A few weekends after Cesare left Milan, he invited me to his hometown for dinner with his family. Apparently, his parents wanted to meet me and get to know me.

It was a perfect night. The air was crisp and fresh. The restaurant itself was beautiful with a veranda that overlooked a view of the city. Cesare's family was lovely and everyone treated me as if I was already a part of the family. I knew that this was probably classic Italian hospitality but still, I was grateful for the warmth and welcome.

Cesare gestured at me to follow him and we headed to the backyard of the restaurant where there was a gazebo and a tune by Einaudi was playing. As we slow danced, in that moment, I felt that nothing and nobody could ever come between us. My stomach fluttered and I was overwhelmed with emotion.

♠: I've always experienced love in a very painful way and that's why I have always been cold and sceptical, believing that love is much more about suffering and less about happiness. In any case, women are emotional and often see issues when there are none. So if the situation calls for it, I will tell a white lie to avoid unnecessary pain.

♦: When he did so, I felt profoundly hurt and told him that I would break up with him.

♠: She always overreacts.

♦: My reaction is proportionate to the pain I felt!

♠: It is not right to rummage through my stuff to see if I did anything wrong.

♦: Hiding your past is wrong.

♠: Inflating the issue is wrong.

♦: It got to a point where I did not trust him anymore and thought that he was hiding something from me.

♠: This is one of the reasons why I've always been wary of love. Love can make you lose control as a result of openness and honesty with your partner. Sometimes, it might be better to withhold certain things.

♦: Love is irrational and I admit that it is not always easy to manage our own fears, which can sometimes transform into unhealthy obsessions.

♠: I've told her many times that we handle situations differently and I don't deal with things the way she does.

♦: I've asked him to open up more and involve me in his life. That's what love is about. It is about compromise and finding a middle ground. It's about not holding grudges and simply enjoying each other's company. Love happens when it does, slipping in to fill the gaps in life with magic. That's how we found each other in the first place.

@inseparable

DIRTY LITTLE SECRET

Don't tell me you don't believe in love at first sight.

The instant you meet someone, either the feeling is there or it's not. There is no in between. If something is there, you can feel it in your stomach, your heart, your throat, and in your brain.

This was our relationship, and no one else's. It's still a very special memory.

We first grew close because he used to love everything I loved. Art, music, engineering, open mindedness, travelling and so much more.

There have been times where I thought there could be something more than friendship between us but I realized he was not generous with me, and he never behaved like he wanted to go beyond friendship.

Instead of waiting and watching, I decided to tell him what I wanted from us. He didn't miss a beat, and started being much more generous and open with me. I had no idea it could be so simple!

Initially, everyone around us believed we were only friends but little did they know that I was going to his place at night and slinking out of his window every morning.

@mental harmony

I believe that what made our relationship so special was the incredible mental harmony and understanding between us. We could spend hours in bed, as if we had all the time in the world, and we could talk about anything that came to our minds, no limitations or restrictions.

Unfortunately, our sexual connection was nowhere near our mental connection. Even though we had a lot of fun together, and our love and our connection was absolutely unique, we just couldn't satisfy each other sexually.

Was it our rhythms? Was it the shape of our bodies? Was it our expectations? I had no idea, and I couldn't even explain it. The only thing I knew was that sex was neither fulfilling nor satisfying for us.

We turned to other sources of satisfaction. We would look for people who had no intellectual connection to speak of with us, but could satisfy us sexually. He knew everything, as did I. I would tell him about my encounters and he would tell me about his.

No matter how normal you try to describe it, there was nothing normal about it, especially when you're living through it.

He would become aggressive when I told him about my romps, and I would fall into a spiral of jealousy when he told me about different girls.

He was an extremely smart person and he knew that this was going to destroy us.

And that was indeed what happened.

@erasmus

After this continued for a while, we begin to feel like strangers. We still would look at each other in the eyes, but we did not connect anymore. The intense and beautiful love was fading, even against our own will.

I decided to leave for Erasmus in Europe – and he was not happy about it.

He explained that he was missing me in such a strong way that he felt dead inside without me. I knew exactly what he meant.

But while he was suffering and his heart was breaking into pieces, I was busy living my new life in that new country. Everything was a discovery, new friends, new food, new university. I simply did not have time to feel sad or think about what I had left behind.

Once I returned from my Erasmus, he left for his Erasmus with the clear intent to make me go through what he suffered through. What goes around comes around, as they say.

@the end

While I understood why he did it, I could not tolerate nor overlook his lies.

He used to call me to make me worry, by feeding me tales about an elusive thief on the beach, a group of gypsies who broke into his house, a bout of salmonella because of fish he had eaten straight from the ocean, an almost deadly fall from a horse…

The lies went on and on and on.

How did I know he was lying to me? I had my spies, close mutual friends. He was now making me pay, that was all.

I wasn't surprised, because love is not only about happiness and beautiful moments. It can also mean pain, suffering, pride and revenge.

@was this love?

I had asked myself over and over if this was real love or not. The answer has always been yes, it was.

After all this time, he remains the only person with whom I've shared every single bit of myself with such unparalleled depth and intimacy. He is still the only person I have had such a strong level of intimacy and intellectual connection.

He is also the only person who has ever been allowed to hurt me so deeply. We were so open and vulnerable with each other that hurting was so easy, so normal.

To tell the truth, I miss that connection. I miss having someone I can create that level of connection with, someone I can show my weaknesses to and be so vulnerable to without judgment.

DREAM

If you think about how love is portrayed in movies, you'll notice the feeling of love is universal.

Because people can't live without love, and this is true for humans all over the world. Humans can live without many things in life, but I don't believe love is one of these things.

@Bahia Espelho beach

A few years ago, I was traveling in Brazil with one of my best friends. We were headed for Bahia Espelho Beach, one of the most stunning beaches in existence.

Bahia Espelho Beach had beautiful sand and sea, but the best part of this island paradise was the difficulty of getting there. It was hidden, secluded, definitely off the beaten track for most tourists.

When we arrived, we realized that there was no hotel, so the plan was to stay there for just one day.

As we sat on the shore, chatting as the waves crashed gently against our feet, I started looking around and my eyes met the eyes of a guy at the bar.

"Who is that guy?" I asked my friend immediately. He didn't know either, so literally five minutes later, we were at the bar. There he was, helping the barman.

"A soda please," I said. That soda was the first of many other sodas and beers and juices. I was clearly flirting with him and I was surprised that no Brazilian model appeared to yell at me for flirting with her boyfriend.

His name was Miguel, a very sensual name. He was the owner of the only bar and hotel in Bahia Espelho Beach.

Change of plans. My friend and I decided to stay a little longer.

That night, Miguel and I went for a long, romantic sunset walk. We strolled hand in hand, enjoying the warm sand in our feet, the cool air on our faces and the beautiful connection in our hearts.

His life decisions fascinated me. His adventurous and free spirit brought him to leave behind what the majority of people call "normality".

He left the big city and his corporate career to live instead in the beautiful and remote Bahia Espelho Beach. This made him feel alive, every single day.

For the first time in my life, time ceased to exist. No day, not night, only me, him and our beautiful connection.

We sat down on the sand to enjoy the sunset. There was no one else, just us. We kissed and kissed. I was in love with him and he was in love with me. There was a connection that cannot be explained.

He sent flowers to my room every single day that I stayed there. The smell of the beach, the taste of the food he prepared for me, the flowers in my room. It was a dream.

FLIGHT OR FRIGHT

As I walked down the streets at Christmastime, after leaving my husband to watch football in the pub with his friends in peace, I mulled about life in London.

In London, you can meet anyone while walking on the road. That's the beauty of London, the fact that you are actually nobody and you don't know anybody.

I stepped into my favorite bookshop and heard a voice from the past.

"I would buy this book instead for...." I knew this voice.

I ducked my face to hide behind my long brown hair to take a look at the owner of that voice.

Just two seconds ago, I had been reflecting on how difficult is to meet someone you know in London.

I couldn't believe it. I ran away from the bookshop, holding my breath as memories from a lifetime ago came flooding back.

@2004

It was 2004. He was in Italy for Erasmus, and he was completely in love with me.
He was a really nice guy, light eyes, light skin and a true gentleman who always treated me like a princess.

We first fell in love in our home, but he decided to go to Italy because that's where his ancestors came from. And so we began a long-distance relationship.

Anyone would warn you about the perils of a long-distance relationship. But somehow, I always believed our love was going to be stronger than anything, even distance.

But while he was in Italy, I started falling for another guy.

@the other guy

I wasn't proud of how I felt, and I tried as much as I could to quell those feelings.

I spoke to one of my university professors, and I still remember what he told me then. "There is absolutely nothing wrong or weird to feel attracted to more than one person."

I met this other guy at the summer party of the year. All my university friends were there and all of a sudden, I found myself kissing one of the guys of the party. When we came up for air, we ran off, leaving the noises of dancing, singing and drinking in the distance.

"Do you want me to kiss you for real? No one needs to know," he told me. I still had a boyfriend, but he was so far away, and I was caught up in the moment with this guy. And yes, I did want him to kiss me for real. Badly.

After that kiss, many other kisses came, and with them came a lot of flowers cards, and gifts, each better than the last.

In this whirlwind of romantic gifts, I also received a present from duty free. From my man in Italy. I instantly knew the connection was gone. He should have known how much I hate presents from duty free.

@déjà vu

Here I was in London, in the midst of Christmas, of the little cozy markets, with the steamy breath and him a few meters from me.

Despite everything, being confronted by the sight him once more re-opened my emotional floodgates. He was every bit as handsome as I could remember, maybe even more.

I still don't know why I reacted like that. It was very instinctive.

Perhaps love leaves a trail inside all of us. It doesn't matter if we think we have left it behind. The trail is always there, and maybe, this proves my professor right.

FREEDOM FROM ME

There are no rules in love. It changes with time, with chemistry, and it never stays the same.

Luckily, I say.

Imagine how boring it would be if it was always the same. If the feeling does not evolve, it means love is actually dead.

The immobility of a love is the beginning of its destruction.

If love was like a career, you'll need to try different things to reach new heights, to keep things interesting, exciting and challenging. Thinking that love is only about happiness would be naïve. It is also about suffering and compromise, in order to achieve happiness.

My love story is a classic example of destiny pushing you to meet the person you are meant to spend the rest of your life with.

@China

I travelled to China for work unexpectedly, when my boss ran into visa issues, and so I had to attend an important conference there on his behalf.

When I entered the conference hall, I looked around for friendly, familiar faces, but instead noticed a guy who didn't look particularly nice. Let's just say he gave me no reason to want to talk to him.

Later that night, the conference organizers invited the participants to dinner, and I ended up chatting with that guy.

To my surprise, we ended up getting on like a house on fire. It had been a long while since I had been charmed by anyone's stories, knowledge and personality.

He hailed from a country I had never been to, and of which I did not know anything more than what Lonely Planet could tell me.

On my flight back, I found myself crying while listening to a love song. I knew I had met my soulmate, but I also knew that we probably would not spend our lives together.

Even though I was certain he was my soulmate, you'd never have guessed it. At first, I didn't even want to be called "his girlfriend."

I was at odds with myself because my life was like a rollercoaster. Life was fun, I was travelling, meeting new people, experiencing new things and this made me want an on-off relationship.

@ultimate test

Months passed, and he demonstrated his great maturity and patience to me when I went through the most trying time in my life.

I lost two family members who meant the world to me. I cannot even begin to describe the kind of depression and numbing sadness I experienced.

It was then that I finally understood he was the only person I wanted close to me at that point.

And so we started over. We started dating with a long-term plan, we were serious about each other and our feelings, and our relationship deepened.

It carried on for years. And while it was not always idyllic, I believe nothing in life truly is.

Everything changes in life. And the biggest difference between any of my past relationships and this one was only me, myself and I.

The relationship I have with love, with myself, with everything – that makes all the difference.

I now realize that the first and biggest writers of our love stories are ourselves.

And I'm completely fine with that.

FULL MOON

@standards

Love is unselfish.

I once dated a guy who really loved me. I knew because he gave me the complete freedom to be myself and accepted me unconditionally.

A connection, a spark. Love is that too.

Many of my girlfriends tell me that they are very happy in their relationships because their boyfriends are kind and nice. Even if the guy has the best character in the world, if there is no spark, there is no love and no relationship. None that will last anyway. That is what I believe.

Connection, honesty and respect. All together in one person.

I have found each of these in different people I have dated over the years but never all in one single person.

Ten years ago, I would have added physical attraction to the list but I realise now that it is not as important as I once thought it was.

I love being in love and it makes me incredibly happy but, like everything in life, there is another side to it which makes me uncomfortable.

Vulnerability.

Love makes a person vulnerable. It makes me vulnerable, allows another person to actually hurt me. It strips away the layer of independence that I build around myself and leaves me defenceless. Eventually, I become paranoid and my irrational side takes over, controlling my thoughts and actions. Everything becomes a worst case scenario and I only see the things that confirm my negative preconceptions.

For my mother, the condition was wealth. She was obsessed with wanting me to marry a rich man. To her, it was an opportunity that she missed out on in life and a mistake she wanted me to avoid.

Ironically, the closest I came to marriage was dating married men. I dated so many that I lost hope in marriage and monogamy. A real commitment requires a strong and rational willingness, the right mind set. People who are not strong enough or in the right frame of mind should not marry. It is not acceptable to fuck around if you are married. Or even if you are not.

@first love @first sight

Richard was my first love and the first person I could see myself spending the rest of my life with.

That summer, one of my best friends knew someone in California who could help us find a job. I did not really want to go all the way there just to find work but I went anyway. One of the hotels in the city centre was looking for someone to take care of the kitchen and we all applied but I was the one who got the job.

I have never been a morning person and I hated waking up early but impossible as it sounds, I managed to do it and missed only 3 mornings in several weeks.

One especially busy day, I was running in and out of the kitchen – the uniform was not only hideous, it was uncomfortably hot, red-faced, and perspiring like I had just run a marathon, my hair a complete mess.

At this very unfortunate moment, I looked up and saw a guy (he was extremely cute) standing in the doorway.

"Hey, hey, slow down babe." His voice was warm and comforting, and I was completely charmed. I stopped right there and we chatted. I don't remember what we talked about but I remember clearly how he looked that day. Tall, confident but not unpleasantly so and he spoke with a toothpick in his mouth like a modern day James Dean.

"Don't leave without giving me your number ok? I want to take you somewhere on the 4th of July."

His invitation took me by surprise. But I was also excited and when my shift ended, I wrote my name and number on a piece of paper before handing it to him.

The next day, I overslept and got to work an hour and a half late. They fired me of course but I hardly felt anything. All I could think of was how glad I felt that I had given him my number in time.

That week, he came to pick me up in a big and black truck. I still remember what he was wearing that night – a white shirt with a dragon on it, and the smell of the perfume he had on.

I was 21. He was 29. And everything was perfect.

We took a slow walk along the shore and sat on a bench by the beach. The moon was full, it was silent and we could see the distant lights of the city spread across the horizon. He put his hand on my knee and my body tingled in response. Later on, when he kissed me, I felt such an intensity of emotion I thought I would pass out. That night, we ended up on a couch at his friend's place smoking weed together.

That weekend, we decided to stay home and spend some time together, get to know each other. And I discovered just how gentle and caring he was.

While watching TV, I took off my shoes and he noticed that one of my socks had a little hole. I was a little embarrassed.

The next day, the owner of the pub where I was working passed me a package. "Some guy left this package for you".

I knew instantly who it was. There was a card along with the package. "I want to take care of you. I thought you might need a new pair of socks. ☺"

I never felt more loved than I did then.

Every week, he sent me something. Small gifts to tell me I was special, to remind me of his presence, so that it felt like he was there in person.

Our connection felt so intense and so deep that there are no words that can properly describe it. The first time we slept together, we both cried like two kids who just discovered how beautiful the world truly was. There were no barriers, no walls between us.

That summer, I decided to move in with him and my family came to visit shortly after. Everyone loved him. They thought he was funny and interesting, it was impossible not to love him. He even won my dad over and I have never seen my dad bonding like this with any of my boyfriends since. The entire visit was amazing and it gave me memories I will remember for life.

We ended up with a long-distance relationship because I was still a student and he was working, and our lives were in two different places. Little did we know that we were also at different places in life and it was a distance that would separate us permanently. He wanted to take the next step, get married, start a family, have kids and a house. But I was not ready.

We stayed together for two beautiful and unforgettable years but in the end, he married someone else.

After his funeral, his wife told me that he never loved anyone else as much as he loved me, not even her. That he had always loved me.

Till today, I have never found another love like the one we had. And probably never will.

@memories @forever love

ITALIAN

Love is happiness. There will still be fights obviously but you go through it knowing that in the end, you will still be able to make peace and return to a state of joy.

The thing about love is that there are no rules. Some people fall in love right away, some start out as friends and stay that way for years before discovering a profound depth of feelings for the other person. You can be more in love with a person than you were a minute before. It can grow or it can fade, and time is never really a good indicator.

@first impressions

The first time I met him, we did not click.

We were having an aperitivo with a group of friends, we hardly spoke and our opinions diverged.

When I first moved to Italy to do my MBA at a prestigious business school, I did not intend to stay long. The plan was to get through the course, graduate and return to my home country. Which is why I decided to continue a long distance relationship with a guy I was seeing then. The prospect of life in a new country filled me with so much excitement that I felt like I could overcome just about anything.

The first few months flew by very quickly and I spent most of it trying to settle in, catching up with my studies and trying to pick up Italian to assimilate better into the Italian way of life.

Around this time, I was invited to a friend's house-warming party in a beautiful historical building in Porta Romana. I was reluctant at first but after much persuasion, decided to go. When I got there and the door opened, the first person I saw was…him. For some strange reason, I found myself smiling despite not wanting to.

It might have been the multiple rounds of gin and tonic that night but I remember that I danced a lot – in the kitchen, in the living room, at the balcony, and I enjoyed every second. After the party, a bunch of us headed to Old Fashion, a club that I did not particularly like. There, on the dance floor, I found myself dancing with him as he drew closer and closer. All of a sudden, I felt like I could not breathe and desperately needed some fresh air. He followed me out and when we got to the entrance, he abruptly kisses me.

@strangers

I still remember our first date as if it had only happened yesterday. He came over to my place at 1am and despite the odd hour, it all felt very natural with him. We talked for two hours without stopping and just like that, we spent the night together.

We were taking it easy. At that time, we did not tell anyone we got together.

Along the way, however, something changed.

The first time I felt that the relationship got serious was when we were in Marocco. He paid for everything except the hotel because I was broke and could not have gone otherwise. We had an incredible trip and after we got back, it felt like we had taken one step further.

For one, it felt like he was treating me officially as his girlfriend.

@different

My family did not approve of me dating an Italian man. Moreover, they wanted me to return home as soon as possible and, even better, to start a family with someone of the same culture and nationality. They refused to accept or believe that I was actually serious about this man.

A year into our relationship, we wanted to visit my family for the holidays. I told my dad about our plans and that I wanted them to meet. My dad agreed but warned me that it was not because he believed this to be anything serious. To him, there could not possibly be a meaningful or long-lasting relationship between two people who grew up in such different countries and with such contrasting background. There was no point in trying to convince him, so all I said was, "Wait and see."

When we arrived, I could tell that my family were happy to see that he was a regular, normal person. Perhaps they had expected him to be some weird Italian rock star or maybe a Casanova, so rich was their imagination.

After the initial relief, they wasted no time in focusing on our now anticipated marriage. Every week thereafter, during our weekly Skype calls, my dad would ask me without fail, "When are you both getting married?" It drove me mad.

His parents, on the other hand, wanted to be part of his life decisions, who he was dating and what were our plans. They believed strongly in the concept of freedom and the right for anyone to live whatever life they chose for themselves.

We met over a beautiful dinner at a restaurant close to the beautiful town square of Florence. Everything went well and we talked about many things. Open-minded and curious, his parents asked me about my culture, my family, and what it was like where I came from. I loved the fact that they wanted to know more about me and answered all their questions happily.

@to be continued

We were on holiday in my home country and it was the best time to visit for the colours, the festivals, the sun and sea, and the never-ending sunsets.

One evening, after coming back from an evening of shopping and coffee, we sat at the balcony, silently and comfortably watching the sun shed its final light. At that moment, unexpectedly, he proposed.

Ecstatic, I said yes.

Even today, my husband remains a person who believes in living in the present, seizing each day as it comes. He lived this way in his own life and in our relationship.

I cannot wait to experience what life brings us but for now, I am just enjoying the moment.

KARMA

Love is completely losing control. It is an emotional state that cannot be controlled, no matter how hard you try.

As we grow up, we become weighed down by doubts, worries and we always end up taking the safest route. We become afraid of suffering, vulnerability, loss and rejection.

But I still think love has no end. For example, if a person in love gets hurt, that person will feel pain and even humiliated, but that person will still be able to love. Call me a dreamer but I want to believe that love for life exists.

The guy I am thinking about complements me and I really believed we could spend our entire life together.

It was kind of our code – We look for each other without ever wanting to know too much about each other. I enjoyed spending time with him and he enjoyed spending time with me. This is enough for us.

And it became a classic situation of how he was such a dear friend, he was almost like a brother.

It was only when, after many years, our relationship became more stable and solid, that we lived the best moment of our whole lives.

@motorcycle

It was a very warm afternoon in Rome. He came to pick me up on a vintage motorcycle from his dad's collection. As we weaved in and out through the charming streets of Rome, I tightened my arms around his waist.
After a while, I tried to move my hands but he reached for them, tightening them around his abdomen again, as the wind whipped against our faces. Amazing. I can still remember it as though it were yesterday.

He slowed down slightly, turned his face to me, and said, "Close your eyes." I could see his eyes smiling through the visor. When I opened my eyes, Castel of the Holy Angel was right in front of me with the stunning sunset sky behind.

That night we went back to his place and we stayed there the whole night, and the whole day after. We didn't want to leave that room. We didn't want the day to come to an end.

We were afraid that the amazing feeling would end once we left.

Nothing had ever happened in our seven years of friendship, but I always felt strong tension between us. You know, that kind of energy that we both knew existed, but swept under the carpet just because we were afraid of losing each other if we talked about it.

In those seven years, I often found myself judging other guys based on him, but obviously with very little success until today. That's life, I guess.

Thinking back, that energy had been there even when we first met, one summer in Morocco. He tried to kiss me then, but we were both young and carefree, we didn't take any of that seriously.

At that time, nothing could have foretold the seriousness of our actions. Karma decided that when he came to visit me in Milan, I would already have a boyfriend and he would be single. I understood he wanted something more, but time was not on our side.

Soon, I broke up with my boyfriend, but he had found a girlfriend. And then they broke up too.

We both couldn't find anyone with such a strong energy and connection. And so, we decided that Karma will take a decision for us.

MEANT TO BE

What is love? For many people, love is all about romance, sweetness and bliss. For me, romance simply isn't everything.

To me, the foundation of love is understanding and accepting – not just your partner, but yourself and your expectations, too. This is the cornerstone of true love, which is why trying to change someone in the name of love is sure to fail. Quite simply, you are yourself, and I am myself.

This is something I hold close to my heart, because after all, my love story was only possible after I was forced to understand true love and let go of what I thought was romance.

@dream come true

It all began with a dream, the dream of living in London. When I first moved to London from Thailand, I felt like a lost little bird. Luckily, I found a home with a lovely, cultured family who opened their home to me and accepted my culture and introduced me to theirs.

Unfortunately, just as I got my bearings in this beautiful city, my hosts had to relocate to Dubai. Living alone in London is indeed a beautiful dream – but only if you're making millions. I was a lowly student, which meant that dream was destined to remain a dream.

I'd met a good friend, who I considered my family in London, along with my hosts. Once he heard that I needed a new place to stay, he didn't think twice before asking me to live with him. We were best friends at university, we were like-minded, we both practiced the Muslim faith, and we loved the same things. We'd enjoy a cone of delicious Italian gelato while strolling along the Thames, we'd have a blast going on shopping sprees in Camden Town, and we loved staring at the stunning sight of the Big Ben – we even saw a shooting star once!

Of course, I was over the moon when he suggested I move in with him and his roommates. I remember that moment as clear as day. It was Christmas Eve, and as soon as I agreed, it felt like I'd made the best possible decision. At his urging, I called my parents to share my excitement over this fantastic news.

It didn't take much for me to fall completely in love with him – completely, head over heels, enthralled, mesmerized and swept up in my very own fairy tale.

@the test

I had a very simple idea of love at that age. As soon we began living under the same roof, we started behaving like a couple. What I didn't realise at that time was that he was actually testing my ability to be a good wife.

Each time he tested me, he spent time teaching me something new, and I naively thought this was love.

He would test my cooking skills, and it was an impossible task for me then – it was all I could do to poach an egg! Not much, I know. But in Thailand, our family had three maids and we'd never even poured the water in our glasses. I'd never imagine that one day, I'd be preparing a meal on my own!

My mum was so surprised when I called her one day asking her how to make chicken curry. After hours on the phone, I was really proud of myself because I managed to cook a meal that looked and tasted great. I was so excited, and couldn't wait to present it to him that night.

He tried it as I beamed in pride and happiness. After one mouthful, he threw it straight into the bin while angrily shouting, "This is not up to my standards!" I hid my hurt and mortification, while apologizing profusely and promising that I'd do better next time.

He also tested my housekeeping abilities, and he started with teaching me how to iron properly. Once I fell short of his strict standards while ironing his shirt, and he bit off my head, saying, "You'd better iron properly next time, this is not up to the standards I taught you." Again, I apologized and promised to do better next time.

Another time, I was ill and resting in bed. Wanting to wake me up, he threw a bucket filled with ice and freezing water onto me. It was so traumatizing, I honestly thought I was going to die.

But I thought this was love.

When he proposed, I was beyond excited. I just couldn't wait to get married to my love, for our love.

Before we could get married, we needed the approval of my parents, and so we travelled all the way to Thailand to meet my parents. My dad asked him where we would live, and he said, "UK, obviously." My dad was satisfied by his answer, and told us, "Good answer. Your home country is not the right country for my daughter."

After a blissful week in Thailand, we came back to London, and he gave me the engagement ring that his mother had given to his father years ago. It was a rather masculine ring, but I didn't care – I was in love, and that was all that mattered.

We waited and waited in the UK for our visa, but unfortunately, it never came. This meant one thing – our life was going to be in his home country. I was devastated by the turn of events, and called my mum in tears, sobbing and crying without saying a word.

Finally, my mum comforted me. She said, "Let's go to there. Let's check the situation, and then we'll decide what to do together."

We arrived in his home country, and he introduced me to his two mothers. He wasn't affectionate towards me in front of them, but then, he'd never been loving towards me even in London, so I didn't think anything of it.

But then, everything began to unravel.

@turning point

That night, he told me, "I could easily marry someone ten years younger than you, but at least you're beautiful, so it's fine." I couldn't understand why he would say something like that to me.

When my dad asked him about how we would live in that country, he explained that I would not be allowed to drive or work. That was the deal if I wanted to live there with him.

Knowing my dad, he would never accept this for his daughter. He rang up a close friend who was a Vice President in an international company, and he was relieved to hear that women could work, especially in MNCs, who always welcomed foreign talents.

We then decided to go for ride with my future husband and understand our future life together better. My dad asked, "If you don't have much money, would you send your children to school?"

My future husband said, "Why should I send them to school if I don't have any money?" Once he said that, my dad spoke to me solemnly in our mother tongue so that no one would understand.

"If you marry him, I swear, I will slap your face even though I've never, ever done that before. After that, I will disinherit you. Is that clear?"

When we left his house for the airport, my dad told them, "My daughter needs some time to digest the country, and we will let you know in a couple of days once we are back in Thailand."

That was the last time I ever saw him. Was that love? For me back then, it was. For my parents, it was not.

Today, I can say that I've never been so grateful to my wise and caring family for making me see the light and understand that there was another side of love and happiness which I had yet discover and experience.

@a new hope

The next three years were one of the lowest points in my life. I was single, sad, and completely heartbroken when my mother was diagnosed with a rare and incurable disease.

My cousins convinced me to embark on a new adventure in a singles camp in Kenya. I was unconvinced about the camp, but I was game simply because I didn't have anything to lose.

The first thing I did at the camp was fill in a form about the kind of partner I was looking for. Colour of his eyes. Height. Nationality. Age. Religion. As I was doing that, I quickly noticed that there were significantly more girls than guys, and I knew it would be harder than even I had expected.

I wandered around for a few hours, and suddenly one of the counselors came up to me with a beaming smile on his bearded face.

"I've found a guy for you," he said. I felt a frisson of excitement, and said, "Excellent. Let's set up an encounter."

When the time came to meet the guy, I arrived on the dot at the hotel bar where we were supposed to meet. One hour passed, then two, and finally, it was three hours after. There was still no sign of the guy I was waiting for.

Annoyed at this unexpected rudeness, I stood up to leave. Out of nowhere, the counselor who had been so eager to set us up appeared, imploring me to stay while he called the guy. From a distance, I couldn't read his lips as they were hidden by his beard, but I could see that he was visibly annoyed. He hung up and hurried back to me, assuring me that the guy had been swimming and he'd be right with us in five minutes.

Five minutes later, a guy with dripping wet hair arrived in a slightly wet shirt. We sat down to have a chat, and one of his first questions was the million dollar question – "How old are you?" he asked.

"27," I replied as his face grew surprised, and then visibly fell. We spoke for a few more minutes, and he quickly left.

While I couldn't deny he was intelligent and extremely good-looking, I was appalled by his lack of manners, his lateness and keeping me waiting while he was frolicking in the pool, and his abrupt departure from our table – he left before I had even gotten up from my chair!

The last straw for me was later, when I overheard him telling his friends, "She is too old for me!" Although he thought I couldn't hear them, I heard every single word and my patience dissipated at once.

I left in anger, but the counselor caught me by the hand, telling me to stop and be patient.

It was clear he could see something I couldn't.

We met again that evening alone. No friends from his side, and none from mine.

We had all the privacy in the world, and we spoke openly with tranquility. As I shared the story about my previous love experience, he wept. I was moved by his sensibility and his desire to protect me.

The time we spent together was beautiful.

I liked this new side of him, and I decided to spend more time in Kenya to get to know him.

When we left Kenya, he went back to London and I came back to Thailand. But I knew distance was not my thing, and I quickly moved to London once again – a bet on him, on life, and on love.

@what is love

A new dawn for our relationship began when I moved to London. Our love became much bigger and stronger than the two of us. It was so different than any kind of love I'd felt before.

Because this new love was founded on understanding, acceptance and even mutual compromise.

At first, we were adjusting to each other, like two pieces of a puzzle that had not yet been perfectly cut to fit one another. Slowly, we opened up towards one another's worlds and everything fell into place.

We were married with the love and blessings of my beloved mother, who fulfilled her wish of seeing me get married before the end of her days. Today, I believe she's protecting us with her soul, every single day.

Love has many forms and meanings, but the only one I accept now and the only one which I will teach to my future kids is the one which makes you feel good, happy and confident.

NO PLANS

I realised that I was in love with the idea of being in love rather than with the person himself. For the longest time, I was caught up in the fantasy of what we could have been rather than focusing on the reality of the present.

And the reality was, he was an asshole.

Looking back now, I could see how unhappy I was and how all my birthdays were often incredibly disappointing because of him, a spoilsport. I could not see it then.

After many years, we finally broke up and my friends were ecstatic. They came over to tell me how happy they were for me. It was no surprise but I was touched.

What I got in exchange for those lost years was a lesson to always, always love yourself first. You have to like yourself first before others would, before you can believe that you deserve the best in life and love. Spend time on the things that make you happy and don't waste time on people who do not care about you.

When it comes to love, you should expect to feel butterflies in your stomach. Why not? Always live and love according to what is good for you and not according to another person's expectations or demands.

I may not have known it then but I know it now and it's something I remind myself of every day.

@last minute plans @catching a flight

My work was extremely demanding and I hardly had time to plan my holidays in advance. One time, a group of my friends were planning a trip to Cambodia and asked me to join them.

Right away, I said yes. No hesitation, no plans.

The night before my flight, I was in Shanghai where I partied long and hard even though I knew I had an early morning. I missed my flight due to a major hangover, but thanks to my frequent flyer status, I luckily managed to board on the next one.

I am glad I did because that was the trip where I met him.

@see what the heart sees

Cambodia turned out to be utterly mesmerizing, populated by beautiful temples and warm, welcoming people. We spent a lot of time biking around until the sun set, exploring freely and soaking in the atmosphere.

"You seem to be talking to him a lot," one of my friends observed, smiling.

"Am I?"

I did not notice it.

Our first kiss was as unplanned as the trip itself and gratefully, it was the first of many more to come.

He is the exact opposite of me in almost every aspect but I like to think that this is the secret that keeps our love alive and strong. We are now about to move in together and it is something we are both really excited about.

A lot of times, the best things in life happen without planning. The only thing you need to do is choose what makes your heart happy.

OBSESSION

When I was young, love was about sexual attraction, fighting, making up, breaking up, impulse, warmth and uncontrolled passion.

Growing up, love became much more about comfort. It became a sort of nest, identified by a secret and familiar language comprising silly nicknames and code words that nobody else understands. Being the only two people to communicate with it amidst a crowd makes you feel special.

Love means a lot of different things to different people. I could never be so arrogant as to judge somebody for the way they love or for the person they choose to love. Guys, girls, young, old, western, Asian, African, who am I to judge? Every culture has a different way of living, breathing, thinking, practicing, tasting, experiencing, and sharing it. That's the beauty of it I guess.

When I think about the circle of people and friends around me, I can see that there is a prescribed way of perceiving love. One founded on milestones – finding the "right" person, getting or giving a ring, buying or building a home, getting married in church or maybe not, going for honeymoon, procreating or adopting, bringing up the kids and so on.

The problem with this perception is that when things don't go according to plan, feelings of frustration, anger, hate, panic, anxiety, and selfishness quickly take over.

Rather than set milestones, the way I perceive and live love is rooted in the FEELING itself. It is about bearing witness to each other growing and not letting the milestones or the people around us decide how it should be. Love is about bringing the best out of the people and that can only happen with something real and authentic.

@equilibrium

I decided to venture far from my hometown to discover who I really was.

It might sound cliché and silly but it is true what people say, that "it is only in getting lost that you find your real self". This was very true at least for my very young self and it was a decision which changed my life forever.

I left my hometown with no plans and no job. After a few enjoyable weeks, I was running out of money and so, had to find a proper job. The cost of living was incredibly high; I was just a young guy and not diligent enough to think seriously about saving money.

Eventually, I was introduced to a guy who was looking for a website content developer and offered me the opportunity to collaborate with him. Interestingly, the website was about my home country and featured all the best things to do there. Working on it gave me the chance to discover unexpected facts about my home town which I used to label as "too normal, too boring, not international enough" for me. The irony did not escape me, that what I fought so hard to leave behind had now become a source of income for me.

@intense red wine

I loved it that our office was an open space where everyone was seated together, even the big bosses. One of the bosses, Carlos, was extremely hot and the first time I saw him, I felt a jolt of electricity between us. Every time I saw him from my desk, I felt a surge of overwhelming excitement I could barely control. It was a current that ran under my skin, sending a thrill down my whole body.

Whenever I bumped into him, I ended up doing something silly – I would stutter or get completely distracted and end up going to the bathroom to calm down or sending text messages to my colleagues to divert my attention and calm my nerves.

Most people are afraid to act on their feelings because they fear rejection or worse, the confirmation of unrequited love. I refused to believe that the connection I felt was a figment of my imagination, so I emailed him to ask him out for a drink on the pretext of thanking him for the job opportunity.

Within a few seconds, he replied, *"When and where? Cheers, C"*

@multicultural

"He is a Latino. Don't trust him. He is bullshitting you. He is using you."

"He is a Casanova. He is playing you. You'll get burnt."

My dearest friends were trying to protect me but I did not listen. I could not hear them. I could not let go of the love I felt then. I am not sure if I believe in love at first sight but even after so many years, I cannot think of any other way to describe it.

One night, we went out for drinks after work. He said to me, "I'll bring you to my favourite Mexican place, the one with the best tequila in town! Come with me!" How could I say no? In the small, crowded bar, we sat and we drank. The music was loud, the lights were dim and Carlos moved closer as we talked. I could feel his warm breath in my ear. My body tingled.

After four very expensive shots of tequilas, he kissed me and I returned the gesture, passionately. I was completely lost in love, completely drawn to his sexy and beautiful

Argentinian accent, his contagious self-confidence, his beautiful eyelashes.

What followed afterward involved champagne, flowers, gorgeous boxes of chocolate, fireworks, surprises, kisses and passionate hugs on the riverside and beautiful, beautiful sex.

It was an obsession I could not explain nor could I control myself. Thoughts of Carlos filled my mind and I could not think of anything or anyone else.

We kept our relationship from everyone, which meant trying every single hotel, and trying every single subterfuge we could think of. It was both fun and exhausting.

This continued for months. As our secret meetings went on, friends and colleagues who could not stand to see me in this kind of relationship kept warning me about doing something I would regret. I could not care less and I paid no heed to anything anyone said.

Until one day.

It was a Thursday morning, I remember. I arrived at the office and was going through the hundreds of unread emails in my inbox. I stopped at one that had the subject "*Who did you blow?*".

I clicked twice to open the email.

It was empty except for a YouTube link.
I clicked again and what started playing was a porn movie with Carlos as one of the protagonists.

I was speechless. What shook me wasn't the fact that he was a porn actor but that he had kept the truth from me. The deception and discovery proved too much for me and I decided to leave, turning my back on our crazy, uncontrolled, passionate, obsessive love.

I have never told this story to anyone.

THIS COULD BE FOREVER

"Your kiss stole my heart. I want to see you again…"

This was the first message I saw when I woke up that morning.

I never replied, not for months. I wasn't convinced that the kiss meant anything. It was something I did on impulse without expecting anything serious to come out of it.

In fact, the kiss happened in a gay bar where we ended up because my girlfriend and I got bored as we were walking around the city.

I did leave him my number because I kind of liked him. But the kiss itself was not an amazing kiss to be honest and I wasn't really in the mood for love. A childish conquest maybe but certainly not love.

A few months later, I was sent to India – Bombay, for a project. I discovered Bombay to be a massive city housing more than 20 million people. The pace of life and the sheer density left me feeling insignificant. And I saw how easy it was to feel lonely and lost. I did not know many people at that time, only a few colleagues and some friend of a friend who happened to be there on assignment.

Scrolling down my rolodex, I came across one more person I knew, who was in Bombay at that time – the guy I kissed months ago in Hong Kong. I decided to write him and ask him out for dinner, which ended up at an Italian restaurant in the city centre of Bombay.

The next thing I remember is the two of us waving madly at each other at the central train station in Bombay as I stood at platform 24 in tears.
From that moment on, we met wherever and whenever we could – in Hong Kong, Taiwan, Singapore, Shanghai.

He turned out to be the love of my life and one of the best people I have ever met. The opposite of me, his heart was unwavering and what mattered most to him was the time we spent together. I've always been sceptical and yet, he led me to have absolute faith in our relationship since the beginning. Perhaps he saw something I couldn't, felt something I didn't.

We like to talk about us. It makes us feel more connected. We love to discuss about the fact that this could be forever. His parents don't know about us yet but for us, there is no rush. Our love is rooted in the present and we have plans to move in together.

The future will take care of itself.

PINOT NOIR

Love changes, it grows, it fades, it dies. It evolves.

Try asking a 20 year old girl to tell you what love is. She won't answer you with any kind of long term vision. She'll tell you about passion, enthusiasm and attraction.

But passion is not love. Enthusiasm is not love. Attraction is not love. Falling in love can be easy but staying in love is the real challenge.

I have a box full of old letters, and it's been a while since I went through them. Tonight, my husband and children are away, and I'll sit down with a glass of red wine and go through each one of these treasured memories.

Just to remember what we used to write when there were no phones, no messaging, no emails. When relationships were less planned and less controlled and when less was more, for real.

@hello stranger

When I was in my early twenties, I had a boyfriend who would always do nice things for me, but only because it was the right thing to do.

He would bring me out for romantic dinners, because it was the right thing to do. He would give me fresh red roses, because it was the right thing to do. He would show me fireworks in front of the Eiffel Tower, because it was the right thing to do.

The business school we were attending had a three-month internship requirement, which was supposed to give us an understanding of the work at the beginning of the production chain.
And so I packed up and headed for London, while my boyfriend found an internship in Germany.

I found a job in one of the big fast food chains there. Sometimes, I'd work in the kitchen, frying fries and making hamburgers, and sometimes, I worked as a cashier, chatting to strangers that I would never see again.

"One hamburger, French fries and a regular coke please." This guy in front of me was handsome and charming. He looked cool – and his attitude told me he knew he was cool.

I couldn't help chatting a little longer than usual with him.

That same week, we met again in a pub where they were screening the historic rugby match – South Africa's first match after the apartheid.

I was drinking and laughing and chatting with my friends when I saw the cool guy enter. Before you knew it, we went out to the balcony, and I was fascinated by him and his stories.

He's a backpacker, with a long sexy beard and messy hair to boot. He has been travelling for more than two years across Asia and Russia, and now he was discovering Europe.

"I'm going to grab a pack of Marlboro. Be back soon," he said. I stayed there for a bit, fantasizing about how perfect our first kiss would be on that balcony, with the gentle breeze caressing our faces. I wanted him to stay the night, we could go somewhere else to have another drink or smoke a few more cigarettes.

Five minutes, ten minutes, fifteen minutes…he still wasn't back. I didn't want to look too desperate, but I decided to head back inside to see if he needed rescuing.

To my surprise, I found him asleep on the couch while his friends were still watching the rugby match.

That night, I went back home alone, disappointed but confident that we would see each other again.

My gut was right. We had a beautiful summer fling which was supposed to remain only that – a beautiful summer fling. This was the deal from the start. After that, it'd be school for me, adventure for him.

When summer was over, I went back to Business School and moved into the smallest apartment you could imagine. Friends, parties, long nights, rosé wine, good coffee, life was as I wanted.

@stranger no more

After a few months, I got a call.

"Hi, I am in Barcelona and tomorrow I'll reach you. I wanna see you."

He then moved in my little apartment, and stayed with me for over a month. Living together was bliss. I was studying, he was exploring the city. Sex was great, young and passionate. He was also able to cook and I actually was not.

Unfortunately, a month passes very quickly, especially if you're enjoying it. At the end of the month, he told me, "I have to go to Spain and Morocco, but don't worry, I'll write to you."

At the back of my mind, I'd hoped that living together would change his mind, but I knew he was in Europe to travel. While I wasn't overjoyed by this, it wasn't unexpected.

Three months later, I got another call. "I am in town tomorrow, I want to meet you."

I was fuming inside. Do you really think I am going to open the door to you when all I got was one postcard in those three months? Do you think it is going to be so easy with me? I'm not waiting for you! I am a beautiful grown woman, with plenty of suitors – good-looking, wealthy, smart men from all over Europe can't wait to date me and spend time with me!

The next day, I found him standing at my front door, wearing an ugly jumper made with raw sheep wool. It made him look like a shepherd, funny and cute all at once.

I realized I really missed him, and I couldn't help reaching out to hug him.

We lived together again for another month, only to realize than that he was stuck in Europe because he didn't have enough cash to go home.

At this point, we still weren't together, but we were thinking, "Shit, this is working out pretty well."

He headed to London and found a stable job. We then decided to be together officially, eventually moving in together in London.

One night, we were sitting together on the sofa, sharing a bottle of New Zealand Pinot Noir and watching TV.

I suddenly visualized the two of us at 70, sitting together in serene, comfortable silence.

I wanted to make that picture turn into reality, and so I asked him to...marry me.

Unfortunately he told me not to be silly, it was still too early, even though he was six years older than me.

@all in

This is when I decided to stop my studies for a year and find a job – in his hometown.

He was not happy with this decision but he knew he had to accept it if he wanted to stay with me. And so we moved back to his home together.

I loved living there. It was an amazing life, enjoyable work, fantastic people, and an unforgettable ocean. We had a beautiful life.

I went back home to finish my degree, and when I graduated, I told my mum I was moving to the other side of the world for good. Because she liked him so much, she was happy for us.

And our grown up life together began.

@happy ending

One day a few years later, we were supposed to go to Tasmania, but I felt really sick. He took me to the beach instead, and four years after I first proposed, he asked me to marry him.

In 2001, we got married. 22 years together, it is a quite long time but it does not really matter if your journey is beautiful.

Are we perfect? Maybe yes and maybe not. But for sure, we are happy and in love and this is what matters.

REAL VALUE

When I am with him, I can be myself, I can talk about anything, and I feel incredibly safe. This is how I know it is love and not an ephemeral feeling.

When I was young, I used to have so many different criteria when judging a guy. I had a very long checklist, and I would make sure the guy would tick all the boxes.

But even though we try to rationalize everything in life, love is about chemistry and simply cannot be rationalized or explained.

@family

Family has definitely an impact on the way we think about love. For example some of my friends wanted someone who is wealthier and better off than themselves, because this is what their family taught them to value.

At the opposite end, my parents taught me to look for equal relationships in life, and so, I am looking for someone who can be my partner.

@connect

We were attending the same college in China, with its multi-billion population, you can imagine how many students there were. There were tons of chat groups, message boards, everything to help ease the students and help us to know one another.

We first went out for dinner with some other friends, and this is when we both understood it was a match between us.
One day, he asked me out because he wanted to talk to me about the love he was starting to feel for me. Even though doing it on a chat would have been the easy way out given both our introverted natures, he asked to meet face to face because he recognized the importance of the matter.

When we met, he spoke to me openly about his feelings for me. This is so remarkable for a woman like me and I appreciated it so much, even now.

I've never been a romantic person and I don't expect him to be. What really matters to me has always been his ability to be committed, be serious, be trustworthy and be open unconditionally to my own growth and happiness.

This is when we decided to start our relationship and after just a month, I left to go on an exchange program in Europe. Can you believe so? We started our relationship with distance. Not flowers, rings and other expensive presents people give each other to pledge their love.

I've never placed much value on showy stuff and the most important thing is that he and my family think alike.

@what truly matters

Other people could think very differently. Take my wedding for example. We went to a nice, intimate restaurant. No engagement ring and no fancy dress, because we don't really need all those things to stay with someone who demonstrates how your happiness and fulfillment matters to him.

I don't care about having beautiful wedding pictures if my husband is not a supportive person. I am happy to invest our money in a beautiful holiday both of us want, and forgo the expensive engagement ring.

Support is all that matters. For example, my work required me to move for quite some time out from our home town and he never tried to dissuade me, instead he always supported me.

This is love. This is commitment, and confidence in our future. Love is not a diamond. Love is not money. Love is not status. Love is a journey where both people have the opportunity to grow together while keeping their individuality.

If I had to describe love as an object, it'd be black tea. Black is very normal. Warm, stable, and you can have it every single day.

RULES

From 20 to 28 years old, I dated guys who cheated on me repeatedly. I could not understand why it kept happening to me.

Perhaps it is human nature to choose a course of action that is more comfortable, shorter, faster. We are, after all, lazy beasts in the end and if we could find an easier solution to a problem, we would.

Perhaps it is the natural order of things. I read a book that said if we wanted something deeply enough, the Universe would conspire to make it happen. This does not mean we do not have to do anything ourselves. It has to be a desire behind which your whole body and efforts are aligned.

@balance

I have seen many couples who love intensely but in a way that makes no sense to me, what I call over-love. Overprotecting, over-caring, over-generous, over-giving, over-challenging. I'm sure you know what I mean.

To me, love cannot be this. Love is the balance between two individuals and all the phases they go through together. If one or both persons overdo something, it upsets the balance tremendously.

This is, however, the exact opposite of what many of us have been taught. In our cultures, we are socialized into thinking that a woman's nature is to be overprotective and over-giving to her partner, her kids, while the man is naturally the decisions make and protector of the family.

The good thing is, I am nothing like that and neither is he. And we are perfectly comfortable with that. He and I – we've been told by society that we are not compatible because we belong to different social categories. But we do not believe in blindly following rules that come from a mindset dating hundreds of years ago. There are people who are happy to follow because it saves them from the conflicts of following their hear. In our relationship, we set and live by our own rules, and I would not have it any other way.

@chemical reaction

We literally started with a chemical reaction.

I was working in a big pharmaceutical company and one of my best work friends had just quit. She was my go-to person whenever I had a question, so even after she had left, I called her one evening for help. She did not know that particular answer but gave me the name of a guy in the office who apparently knew everything there was to know about chemical reactions.

I could not put a face to the name at first but eventually, I found out that we were on the same floor and our colleagues called him, perhaps unsurprisingly, the "silent guy". Whatever his reputation, he certainly knew his stuff and he came up with the answer to my question almost immediately.

From that time on, we started chatting, exchanging opinions about projects and even leaving the office together whenever possible where he would give me a ride home on his motorbike. On days when it poured, he would try to protect me from the rain, which was completely futile when you're on a motorbike but I was touched by his gentle kindness.

"You know, I sat in the desk near the entrance for a couple of months and every time you passed by, I could smell your perfume," he told me later on, making me blush.

In the months I got to know him, he fascinated me in so many ways. For one, he seemed to be a culinary virgin compared to me and, up to the point when we met, had never tried wine or even a brownie in his life!

Over dinner one night, I asked him, "So what do you think?" "About what?" he answered. I felt instantly disappointed, thinking that we did not have the connection I thought we had. But he continued almost immediately, "Are you also thinking what I'm thinking?" I smiled and at that moment, I knew this was someone I could and wanted to be with.

@creating new rules

We had various differences — religious, linguistic, social class — which made the relationship somewhat complicated but also more interesting.

My father could not accept the fact that we were dating and he could not accept the fact that my father would not give us his blessings. My father, a lawyer and former policeman, was a man of logic and rules. To him, romantic love was a childish idea that had no place in the real, adult world. Needless to say, it was a tense situation.

One day, he called my father pretending to be a potential client seeking legal counsel regarding an important piece of property, and they arranged to meet. My father is four hours late from his court proceedings. When he finally arrived and saw who his potential client was, he was not pleased to find out that he had been deceived. My boyfriend began his well-prepared speech to make a case for our relationship. After he was done, my father said nothing except, "Are you finished?" and left.

That day, my boyfriend came home and told me what happened. I felt a mixture of shock and pride that he would even pull off something like that and for my sake. It was the first time he demonstrated how much our relationship meant to him, how much he wanted me to be happy, and I truly understood the depth of his love.

@the Universe conspiring for love

A few years later, he asked me if I wanted to get married. I told him that I would never accept a proposal without a real ring. Still, despite my unfulfilled desire for an official proposal, we married without fanfare. On the day of the wedding, he gave me a piece of paper on which he listed the promises he wanted to make to me.

I will buy you a house in front of the ocean, from which we can watch the sunset every day.

I will make you brownies.

I will buy you the diamond ring you want so much.

And a few other things that he knew were important to me.

It has been a few years since and he still manages to find ways to surprise me. Every morning, to wake me up, he would make me a big cup of tea before telling me a joke. Whenever I complained about his habits – as wives often do to their husbands – he would join in and complain about himself too and it always made me laugh. I was impossible to be annoyed with him.

I know my mother loves him and they often hang out together, getting along better than even I do with her. My father, on the other hand, has never spoken to him again since the day of the "deception". We do not go over to his house together nor do we invite him to our place. It is the unspoken rule, my father's unspoken rule.

But this is the life we chose and we continue to live by the rules we have made for ourselves, standing by each other at all costs.

To us, this is the price of love.

SELF LOVE

I'm not sure I know what's love anymore. I thought I did, but now that I've just broken up with my boyfriend, I don't know anymore.

I was studying in Mumbai, on a campus in the south east part of the city. He was working long hours at a big bank and living in the north west area of the city. This was the time in which I though love would make you and other people do things which you would never do if you were not in love.

When it rains in Mumbai, it can go on for days and not even the bravest would leave their house because it's like the apocalypse outside with muddy, impassable streets. But not me. I was too much in love to stay away from him and to wait the rain to stop. It took hours, but once I was at his doorstep I knew I did something fantastic, for me, for him, for us.

I am not sure if I would do that now. I am really not sure if I can find that amount of selflessness in me anymore, without wanting something in return.

We spent six years together, with an inexplicable soul connection. Having that connection with someone at any point in life is a privilege, and it does not happen often to anyone.

But when he asked me to marry him, I came to realize that I loved my independence. I realized I had become unable to do anything anymore unless I knew I would get something in return.

Love is amazing, but self-love is equally amazing. I had reached a point where everything in our relationship became a test – If you do this, it means that we love each other. If you don't do that, it means that we don't love each other. Our love was equated to our sacrifices.

All of a sudden, we had lost the magic of love and it became selfishness. I was no longer making sacrifices for him, because I was going through self-exploration, reinventing myself, facing my insecurities, opening up to people, knowing my limits and pushing them.

My priority became discovering myself instead of planning for our future together. I didn't want to speak to him on the phone, because I was constantly busy and I was never around. I knew that it was me.

We still cared about each other, but deep down, I knew it was just a safety blanket. Our love had transformed into a fear of falling out of love and letting go of that amazing safety blanket that I had with me for many years.

We became distant, cold, strangers and we silently split up.

I came to realize that love became so much deeper after that experience.

I was no longer worried about making a good first impression. Love became about caring, rather than perfection, because true love is unconditional. It is driven by physical and mental attraction, by the appreciation of your partner's interests, the desire to support and protect all at once.

Above all, it is driven by vulnerability. Showing, sharing, opening up your vulnerabilities is one of the biggest gestures of love that anyone can show.

Just be willing to be silly, to have your little connections that nobody else will understand, to share your weak spots, to allow the other person to touch you.

That is love.

SHE'S THE ONE

Love makes everything better.

When you love someone, you don't need to understand how you have got to love that person. You can't rationalize it because you don't really get to choose who you love.

You love, because you love, and that's it.

I believe the most unique part of my love story comes from the fact that we needed to get out of our own country to discover our love.

@boundaries

I've known her since we were in our young, university days, and I've always been impressed by her.

I always had this impression of her. She was very clever, the way she talks, the way she communicates, the way she gestures with her hands, always made me think that she was incredible.

Her commitment to everything she does caught my attention so many times, and she was an inspiration for me. I could sense she was special, but at that time she was dating someone else. And this someone else happened to be my best friend.

That's an unwritten universal rule that I abide by – anything more than platonic never even crossed my mind, because she was my best friend's girl. Their relationship lasted two years, and in the meantime I had moved to Singapore, without really thinking about them too much.

I went home for Christmas and met both of them at a party, and I took the opportunity to ask him if he was still seeing her. He was not, and I was surprised and to be honest, I wasn't ready to hear that.

@closer

This was a difficult time for her, and I offered to be her shoulder. She could come to me for any kind of support she needed. Anything at all.

Thanks to this, we became closer, closer and closer. It's strange how difficult experiences can draw people so much closer.

Because she worked for a consultancy company, she had the opportunity to travel the world for work, and she decided to take an assignment in Australia.

I was still living in Singapore, and all that stood between us were a few hours. We didn't miss this golden opportunity, and quickly booked flights to the island paradise of Bali.

If you've ever been to Bali, you'd know it's a special place, almost magical. We went to the beach, we had dinner, we even had massages together. But we had kind of promised ourselves to remain friends.

But at the back of my mind, I knew something was happening. There was something intriguing about her.

"Let's have a beer?" she asked. The club is full, and everyone around us was dancing non-stop. When we got to the bar, I immediately kissed her softly on the cheek. I told her that

I could stop doing that because she needed a friend, but she looked at me, wide-eyed, and asked, "Really?"

The tension between us was mounting and the distance did nothing to help. She would tell me about her dates, and I would listen without asking too many questions.

The tension reached its peak and I just couldn't deal with it. I flew straight to Perth to see her, and we went to a fantastic concert that night. I couldn't help myself, so I kissed her and I slept with her that very night.

After that unforgettable night, we immediately started talking about love. She told me she had three rules for any guy:
1.   She has to be in love with him
2.   She has to know him for more than a month
3.   Her parents have to know him

Check, check and check! Things were looking good for me.

She reminded me that I hadn't really checked the first rule, and so, being a confident guy I told her, "Give me a week, and you'll see!"

@Melbourne

And so we headed for the Great Ocean Road in Melbourne. If you have never been there, you should.

It is absolutely amazing.

We got tattooed together, a cute little aeroplane. She had told me about this tattoo before, and I just decided to get it with her.

We also made a bet, and because she lost, I asked her to write something for me. When the time came to say goodbye, I thought she had completely forgotten about our bet, but she surprised me giving me a letter.

The letter was rich, she explained what she liked about me and what she did not like about me. The letter finished with a nice note. Congratulations, you made me fall in love with you in a week.

At that point nothing seemed fitting other than the three little words.

"I love you."

Then it came. A soft, eagerly anticipated, "Me too."

Everything was magical but there was a problem, and I couldn't stop thinking about it. There was no future for us.

She had her own job, her own projects, there was no space for me in her life.

But I was underestimating our love, because she made space for me. She asked to be sent in New Zealand again for a prolonged period, to increase the time we could spend together.

The distance made us much more creative. For example, for Valentine's Day, I booked a limo and the driver drove her to a romantic restaurant, where she had dinner with me on Skype.

What's next for us? Who knows?

Some people might think I am crazy, while others might think why not go after an easier life and love story?

But for me, if something that I feel is important entered my life, I have to be courageous, I cannot let it go, and I have to commit to it with my mind and soul.

TO BE CONTINUED

Time: 00.45
From: Lucas
Subject:

Hi Sophie, how are you? I wanted to let you know that I am divorcing from my wife.

Need to see you as soon as you can
With love, always yours
Lucas

Tuesday night was one of the most turbulent nights of my life. After reading that email, I woke up in the middle of the night at least three times, shaking with fear and overcome with a horrible, horrible sensation.

I knew exactly why all this was happening. My past was coming back to haunt me, and I dreaded making choices I didn't want to make and facing feelings that I wasn't ready to face.

@Côte d'Azur

He's one of *those* guys. Incredibly good looking, the type any girl would fall in love with at first sight. Or at least, feel the urge to bed him, kiss him, or touch his beautiful sculpted body.

We first met in a bar in the south of France. Nothing happened the first time we met, even though I'd really, really hoped that something.

The next time we came across each other, he was dancing with another girl, with their bodies far too close together. I boldly declared to my friend, "I'm going to get rid of that girl." Not a second later, I headed for him, waving urgently as if I had to tell him the most important and pressing news ever.

I literally stole him from her and I'm not even ashamed to admit it. I believe that when you want something, you need to go and get it. Even if this means kicking some girl out along the way.

The third time, we were at another party, six weeks after I'd stolen him from that girl. The party was fun, but not as much fun as kissing him would be. I'd been trying to get in touch with him since our last encounter, but he never made the effort to reciprocate. When I saw him at the party, I thought he had lost interest.

But I thought wrong. I was dancing with a few friends, and I left for the bathroom. I was washing my hands when I looked up and saw him waiting outside. For me.

Once I reached him, he enveloped me in his strong arms from the back. I was rendered powerless. I instinctively turned slowly to face him, staying in his arms and holding them firmly. I could feel his muscles in my hands, and I could not loosen my grip.

We stared into one another's eyes for few seconds, and we started to kiss with so much passion that my entire body was shaking.

The loud house music from the DJ, the singing, laughing and dancing from everyone at the party faded into oblivion. In that moment, we entered our own dimension. It was only me and him, kissing, clinging on to each other. So tightly.

That night, we walked home under the stars, hand in hand. It was a scene straight out of a Hollywood rom-com. The weather was freezing so I put my right hand inside his pocket to keep it warm with his left hand.

The sex that night was unforgettable. The perfect combination of love, winter and passion. I dreamt about it, reliving it for the next three months.

@love in the air

After that night, the most prominent feature in our love story was airports.

We lived in different European cities, and we spent the weekends shuttling back and forth. The pain of separation was frustrating and I couldn't do it anymore.

When I dropped him off at the airport one evening, I told one of the biggest lies of my life. It was the only way to end the constant pain of separation.

I gritted my teeth and told him that I had stopped loving him, and that I didn't want to see him anymore.

The minute the words left my mouth, I turned my back on him and drove all the way back to London. It was pouring as though the sky was crying for us too, and I was crying inside, desperately in pain.

I spent the next few weeks in extremely pain. I thought I was stronger than this. But I wasn't. I tried everything to numb the pain – smoking, cooking, you name it. Nothing worked. I was still dreaming about the awesome, gorgeous guy I loved and left. His beautiful body still haunted me every time I closed my eyes.

@a new summer

Finally, summer arrived. For me, summers are the best for new beginnings. Everyone becomes relaxed, and anything can happen.
One night, I reluctantly followed some friends to a party, thinking I'd leave as soon as I got a chance. Once we arrived, one of my friends winked as she put a sticker over my left breast, "That tells everyone that you're single, and you'd like to have sex."

As the party became more fun, the music became louder, some of my friends started disappearing. I grabbed a beer, hoping I'd see at least one of them somewhere.

And there he was. Marc, just a few meters away.

But he's not alone. He's talking to a girl. Who is she? Damn, I wanted to get rid of her

Déjà vu washed over me as the same scene played out.

@the nice guy

Marc was the ultimate nice guy. The guy you can count on, the one who takes care of you when you need it the most, the one who will never let you down.

When I was younger, I never treasured guys like Marc. Back then, in whirlwinds of passion, fun, YOLO moments, carpe diem experiences, nice guys like Marc are left behind.

Month after month, when we were together, Marc did amazing and beautiful things for me. Our love story was like a fairy tale. I loved him and he loved me, maybe always a bit more than how much I did.

Month after month, our love became more and more beautiful, we were exploring each other, and beneath his nice guy demeanor, I discovered someone who surprised me in many ways, many times.

But I'd reached a point in my life where I craved experiences that pushed me beyond my comfort zone. I wanted to move to Cambodia and nothing could stop me, not even Marc.

Marc knew he had no chance of changing my mind, so he made a photobook of our memories together, to make sure I wouldn't forget him. I cried all the way to Cambodia, overwhelmed by self-destruction.

Soon, I came to know life in Cambodia. Cambodia was a lovely place, but had no infrastructure or service to speak of. People peed and pooped on the street. They lived in dirty huts without any kind of protection or access to clean water. I stayed in a cramped tiny room with many other people, I only had a bicycle to get around on rundown streets, and I got used to not having anyone understand me.

I went there to help, but I quickly realized how powerless I was in the bigger picture. I threw myself into helping the people there, alienating myself from the life I had left behind in Europe – trivial, meaningless baggage.

Meaningless baggage that included Marc. I went into town and paid for internet access, and I wrote an incredibly nasty email to Marc. I don't know why, but I told him that I was not physically attracted to him, I was not in love with him and I didn't miss him while I was living in Cambodia. There would be no future for us.

Before leaving Cambodia, I took three weeks to travel the country, take in its beautiful sights and think about what I wanted to do with my life.

All of a sudden, Lucas came back into my mind. I had to get him back. My feelings for him never really went away, not even when I was with Marc.

I had dinner with Lucas once I arrived back home. Dinner turned into four magnificent months together.

But my ability to love two people strongly and passionately at the same time reared its ugly head again, and I began dating Marc behind Lucas' back – until Marc asked me to marry him. I wanted him but I didn't really want him enough, and that ship sailed for Marc and I. He married another girl, who had become pregnant only after a few months.

In one fell swoop, I eliminated both of them from my life. Or so I thought.

@once more

Six years later, I saw Lucas again at my best friend's wedding. I couldn't believe my sight – there he was, with his wife and children.

All my lingering feelings rushed straight to the surface, straight to my head. I wanted him so badly but I couldn't do anything.

When his family left the wedding early, Lucas came over, visibly drunk. He tried to kiss me. Though I was drunk and even though I really wanted him, I pushed him away.

I couldn't believe this was happening again after all this time. We weren't even in the same country as before, but nothing mattered because love clearly doesn't know geography nor time.

I went home for Christmas, and as I walked down the familiar streets, I saw him with his family from a distance. I didn't have the courage to face them, and so I avoided him.

I toyed with the idea of writing him a sentimental, reconciliatory email but suddenly realised I didn't even have his email address. Clearly a sign from the universe telling me to stay away.

Two days later. A message arrived. Lucas. A crisis in his marriage. Would like to meet you again.

@something new

What came next was something new for me. We started seeing each other again, beautiful dinners, beautiful words, beautiful things, everything was beautiful.

He was technically still married, but in the midst of divorcing and I was ok with that. But the situation imposed boundaries that we could not – and did not - cross.

I still remember the excitement was growing inside us. It was a beautiful kind of lovely – passionate – hot – friendship. We didn't sleep together, and we often found ourselves hugging, smelling, and enveloping each other on a bench of the quiet fish port in our hometown, as though we were teenagers again.

After two months of "teenage" dating, we had to try. One evening, he finally came up to my place. We were talking, and then all of a sudden we were laying down on the bed.

Everything moved so quickly. I tugged off his pants, and he eased my dress off over my head, but when the situation really heated up, we realized that we could not do it. He still had his wife and children waiting for him at home.

This wasn't going to work. When we kissed goodbye that night, I stood there thinking, Lucas is leaving my life forever.
I was exhausted by all this craziness.

I decided to take three months off, to think, to stop, to reflect, to re-balance myself. I took off for Southeast Asia, where I stayed in beautiful places, met wonderful people, and unlike my previous experience in Cambodia, I was now a grown woman and I knew that I could not escape from my real life or the real me.

While I was travelling, Marc resurfaced and wrote to me to tell me that he had divorced from his wife. He was coming to Southeast Asia to take a break, and insisted that we meet in El Nido, a lesser known paradise in the Philippines.

What happened between us in paradise, I' ll leave to your imagination. Sunrise beach breakfasts, sunset cocktails, midnight skinny dipping – I can't remember a single thing that did not work. Marc had grown up as well, he'd become a mature, attractive, self-assured gentleman.

But all this just wasn't enough. It was never going to be enough to take us to the next level, even after ten years. This time, we both knew it. Our fantasy weekend in Philippines remained our own private secret.

Life went on. Work, friends, life was finally calming down for me. But as usual, I was wrong.

That Tuesday morning, I checked my email…Lucas.

To be continued.

TOO EARLY

Most people have some idea of what real, romantic love is but I don't. It confuses me. A sensation that has no rational explanation – like a strange, unknown animal or a primitive connection - primordial, inexplicable and, at times, unmanageable bond between 2 individuals.

Yet, we often try to rationalise it. Other times, we try to quantify it, defining it by its tangible manifestations – the size of a diamond, the grandeur of a wedding, the price of a house, the number of messages sent in a day and on and on.

@unexpected @new sensations

My university years left me with a collection of memories including the time I fell from my bike on the way to my exams and the day I went for a microeconomics paper right after a night of cheap mojitos and dancing till 5am.

Of all that I remember, one moment stood out as if it had just happened.

I was a third-year statistics major and disdainful of the freshmen who had yet to realise the importance of taking things seriously. One day, just as the lesson was about to start, I noticed a guy entering the classroom, accompanied by one of my best friends.

The minute I saw him, something clicked inside me. I had to get to know him. My heart gave me no other choice. Objectively speaking, he was not the best looking guy at the university but yet, I was attracted to him so strongly it was impossible to ignore. Getting to know him became my mission that semester.

Naturally, I asked my best friend for information but he warned me to stay away as this was a person who didn't have his head in the right place. Unfortunately, it had the opposite effect. I was now more determined than ever to become his redeemer.

The Universe must have heard me because without planning it, we both ended up in the same study group. I found him to be smart and interesting although a bit spoiled. The more time we spent together, the more my feelings for him grew and the deeper we connected. We could read each other with one look and sex was great.

@love button

We were similar in many ways. Like me, he was someone to whom relationships were sacred and we would have done anything to protect what we had together.

Despite the depth of our feelings, it took me a while before I could tell him I loved him. I remember his reaction to my lack of reaction when he said the magic words to me and his insecurity even made me laugh. But still, I could see us growing old together, complete with the big, luminous house by the sea. I knew we would have two cars, which we would use to bring our kids to school before heading to a job we loved.

In reality, we would invent our own recipes with whatever we had in our fridge; I was obsessed with the smell of clean clothes, fresh coffee and long breakfasts in the morning.

I was also obsessed with his happiness and I wanted him to nurture the friendships he had. So when he told me that he was going to Barcelona for a while with his friends, I felt really supportive. I was still hanging out with my girlfriends on weekends and I was glad that he was spending time with his friends as well.

He called me one night while he was there. As we talked, he told me that he was lying down on the sand and it was cold but the sky was amazing. It was so thick with stars that it outshone the moon and lit up the night. I remember thinking to myself, love really did make everything look and feel and sound so much more poetic.

Once he got back, however, something changed. I don't know what exactly or how but I felt a distance between us – deliberate and isolating, as if he wanted to protect me from something. Hoping that it was just a phase, I did not press him and several weeks passed but nothing changed. After years of an amazing and intense relationship, I couldn't believe that things were falling apart.

One night, we tried to make love but he told me he could not because he did something wrong and he couldn't bring himself to be intimate with me. We did not sleep that night. We talked and he told me that he had a one night stand with a girl in Barcelona. He said it did not mean anything because he found real love and that was with me. But I had appeared too early in his life; real love came too early. He was still too young and wanted to explore life, get to know himself and what he really wanted.

So we broke up.

The pain was like nothing I'd ever experienced. Not even when I'd previously lost important people in my life. It felt like a part of me died along with the relationship.

When a truly deep relationship ends, the heart and mind – still in love, struggle with a reality that is almost impossible to decode and digest. So, you try ways and means to cope. You go out with friends, talk to random strangers, drink, fuck someone else, sleep with a woman, bury yourself in work, travel to different countries, volunteer, skydive, anything that could erase the memories or substitute the pain with physical gratification no matter how temporary.

But nothing works.

So tell me, where do I find the stop button?

WAR AND PEACE

I was carrying a load of bombs with a dozen of army companions.

We were heading from Villacidro to a bomb deposit in the nearby San Gavino. The streets between Villacidro and San Gavino were not paved yet, and it was very common to meet people along the way.

Those days, carrying bombs from town to town on streets filled with civilians was nothing out of the ordinary. A different time, as my children and grandchildren say to me.

@zippole

That fateful day, we drove past a group of Sardinian women dressed in ankle-length skirts, carrying heavy and bulky baskets on their heads. Sardinian women are known to be pillars of strength. They are used to helping their families from a young age, making huge physical and mental sacrifices.

We had a few empty seats in our truck, and we slowed down as we neared the group of women. We called, "Do you want a lift?"

The women burst into peals of laughter. They had beautiful smiles and their eyes lit up, filled with of joy. It had been months since I had seen such beautiful women. Being in the army makes you forget the joys of life, and all my memories from a lifetime ago came rushing back at the sound of their joyous, contagious laughter.

The eldest woman was clearly the least enamored, and she threw us a suspicious look. After looking us all in the eye, she accepts our offer.

The wind was very strong, and the roads were rough, so carrying a conversation with the girls was almost impossible. I try anyway.
"What's inside your baskets?"

The elder woman answers, "Carnival season is approaching, so we are bringing home all the ingredients to make *zippole*." *Zippole* is a traditional Sardinian carnival pastry made of soft pasta, which is fried and then sprinkled with icing sugar. Delicious, sweet, savoury, and very nutritious.

My mouth began to water at the thought of homemade *zippole*, the fragrance of fried pasta and the taste of icing sugar.

As soon as she has answered my question, she turns her gaze to the landscape, firmly signaling the end of our conversation. I then try to speak with one of the younger girls, Bella. The elder woman stares intently into my eyes, warning me, "Don't touch her."

"Give him a slap if he deserves it," she then tells Bella. At that point, it was clear to me that I was intruding, but I simply could not care less.

@Bella

Once we arrive at San Gavino, we leave the huge truck. I talk to Bella as we make our way into town, and conversation flows. She tells me that her parents were cooking up a homemade feast, and urges me to come in, because I simply cannot miss the opportunity to try some of their delicacies.

I entered Bella's home, and was greeted by the sight of a man with a hat on his head, a cigar in his hand, sitting on a straw chair clearly worn-out by time.

As soon as he notices my presence, he demands, "What are you doing in my home? You are from the military and you should not be here."

I was immediately annoyed. I hated being treated like an intruder. Everyone should treat each other with respect, especially for the military who are breaking their backs miles away from their families, risking their lives for the war and honoring their country.

"Have you never seen someone from the military?" I counter testily. Although I was frustrated at having to talk to this stubborn mule, I have to admit that this encounter changed my life.

I asked him if Bella was already engaged, and I learned that she was only 17 years old.

Fatefully, right when I asked Bella to be with me, the captain sent me to Turin, without even giving me the chance to see her one last time to explain.

@limbo

The second I could, I wrote her a letter to explain. I was terrified that my letter would never find its way to her. I was terrified that her parents would find it and trash it.

Finally, I received Bella's reply. Relief washed over me. Over the next two years that felt like an eternity, our relationship grew with each correspondence.

We used to share pictures and we would tell each other our stories, our thoughts, and our love.

When the war finally came to an end in 1946, one of the commanders who thought highly of me, wanted to deploy me to Sicily. I vehemently fought my corner, until I could return to Quartu Sant' Elena in Sardinia.

From that moment on, our love would no longer be a simple correspondence.

@life begins

I took a leave of absence to spend time with her. We got married when she was only 19. Getting married at 19 is illegal, but the priest of the church in town knew our families and us very well, so he blessed us and allowed us to marry anyway.

I quickly found a job and we left our parents' houses. In the blink of an eye, we grew to a family of eight healthy, smart kids in a house with many floors.

That very day, that fateful encounter spawned a lifelong love that evolved into something bigger than us. It became a love that lasted almost seven decades, and has begun regenerating through the love of all the families born out of our love, which began so casually on that day like many others.

Acknowledgments

A special thank goes to the editors' passion and talent, the talented designer of the cover Valeria Pola, whom shared their life story with authenticity and openness, and whom also encouraged and inspired me to complete this personal project.

The money raised from the sold copies of this book will be donated to support NGOs devoted to the education and care of children in South East Asia.

About the Author

Silvia Olla was born in Sardinia, Italy, in 1985 and she currently works in Singapore. Her lifelong passion for writing, art and creativity brought this first book to life.

Printed in Poland
by Amazon Fulfillment
Poland Sp. z o.o., Wrocław